SECRET LIVES OF BRITISH BIRDS

To my mother, Charmian Couzens, for years of encouragement
and for launching my love of wildlife and birds in the first place.

for birds
for people
for ever

The RSPB works for a healthy environment rich in birds and wildlife.
It depends on the support and generosity of others to make a difference. It works with bird and
habitat conservation organisations in a global partnership called BirdLife International.

If you would like to know more about the RSPB, visit the website at www.rspb.org or write to:
The RSPB, The Lodge, Sandy, Bedfordshire, SG19 2DL; telephone 01767 680551.

Photographers (by page number)
Bill Baston: pp17, 18, 23, 66, 127
Bram Fey: p129
Chris Gomersall: pp12, 17, 24, 36 (both), 46, 48, 87, 89, 99 (top), 111 (bottom), 113, 115, 122, 134, 136, 137, 151, 153, 156
Yann Kolbeinsson: p149
Rebecca Nason: p30
David Tipling: pp93, 102, 142
Markus Varesvuo: pp6, 15, 25, 35, 37, 54, 62 (top), 64, 69, 71, 77, 86, 96, 99 (middle and bottom), 109 (top), 111 (top), 139, 155
Steve Young: pp28, 40, 43, 47, 50, 56, 60, 62 (bottom), 75, 80, 91, 104 (both), 105, 109 (bottom), 121, 123, 141, 148, 154
Front cover: Barn Owl (David Tipling)

First published 2006 by Christopher Helm, an imprint of A & C Black Publishers Ltd.,
38 Soho Square, London W1D 3HB

Copyright © 2006 text by Dominic Couzens
Copyright © 2006 illustrations by Peter Partington

The right of Dominic Couzens to be identified as the author of this work
has been asserted by him in accordance with the Copyright, Designs and Patents Act 1988

ISBN-10: 0-7136-8280-9
ISBN-13: 978-07136-8280-9

A CIP catalogue record for this book is available from the British Library.

This book is produced using paper that is made from wood grown in managed, sustainable forests.
It is natural, renewable and recyclable. The logging and manufacturing processes conform to the
environmental regulations of the country of origin.

www.acblack.com

Designed and typeset by Paula McCann

Printed and bound in Milan by Rotolito

10 9 8 7 6 5 4 3 2 1

SECRET LIVES OF BRITISH BIRDS

Dominic Couzens
Illustrated by Peter Partington

CHRISTOPHER HELM
LONDON

Contents

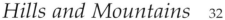

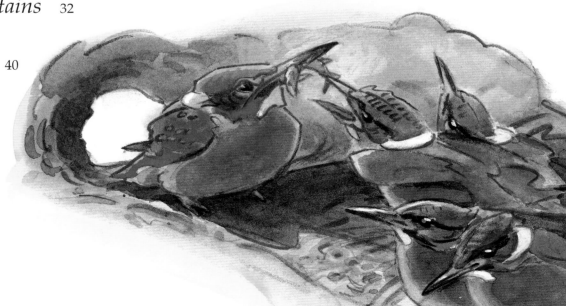

Introduction

MANY PEOPLE love the birds in their garden with a passion and remain content never to take their interest beyond their own private sphere. Others, though, find their thoughts and curiosity wandering with their avian visitors. Slowly at first, and then with more urgency, they begin to wonder where their garden Goldfinches disappear to in the winter, or where the gulls that fly over their house in the evening go to roost. Such people are in the process of leaving their ornithological nest – fledging, if you like. Soon they will find themselves taking their first bird-watching steps into a new environment: exploring a nearby woodland, perhaps, or visiting a local lake to do more than just feed the ducks.

New horizons bring new questions. In the first book of this series, *Secret Lives of Garden Birds*, I tried to reveal how complex and surprising are the lives of those everyday birds that we thought we knew well. The process continues in this book, but something else arises, too. It turns out that many of Britain's habitats – the places where birds live – hold their own secrets. Who would believe that the great expanses of moorland in Northern England or Scotland are not natural, but actually created by humans? And who would guess, while observing the teeming masses of birds that populate our winter estuaries, that the mud and sand would be virtually emptied come the summer?

This book, therefore, is about how our birds fit into all those different parts of the countryside.

It reveals which birds are found in which places, and why. At the same time, all the inhabitants have their own stories to tell, a selection of which appears in these pages. Some are light-hearted (the oversexed frenzy of the Capercaillie); others are very dark indeed (sibling murder in a Golden Eagle eyrie). Some stories happen mercifully free of our influence, while others tell of how we humans have shaped the fortunes of the birds around us.

Everybody, from the confirmed garden bird-watcher to the enthusiast who roams the globe in search of feathered rarities, has a part to play in the fate of our birds. That is the sobering reality of life on our island and, to an extent, around the entire globe. We might think that our only sphere of influence is the garden; but more and more the world of birds is one that revolves around us and is ultimately under our stewardship. Britain, you might say, is rather like a gigantic garden and we are its guardians.

It matters a great deal, therefore, that we are informed guardians, because that is usually the first step towards being responsible and caring ones. And the more we know and care, the better it will be for the fortunes of those creatures with which we share our space. This book, I hope, will play its part in making you informed. That's the easy bit. The caring is harder, and ultimately more exciting and exhilarating. Where it leads is up to you.

HEATHS
& MOORS

Ancestral landscapes

STEP OUT onto a heath or moor and you are walking into a paradox. The landscape here, all rolling heather and wide horizons, seems completely timeless and unbowed to civilisation. The wind-blown gullies of moorland and stark sandy hollows of heaths look like the scars of an ancient conflict between the elements; a battle at which humans are but recent spectators. But, as so often in nature, things are not what they seem. Heath and moor are both habitats of our own creation, exposed over the last few centuries by the felling of the great forests that once covered the land.

HEATHLAND AND moorland are twin habitats, both fashioned from the same dominant plant, heather. "Heathland" is the commuter-belt version, with its mild-mannered climate, pleasing, tree-lined edges and sandy soil that feels so pleasant to the toes. "Moorland" is the more rugged northern version, with its wild, treeless vistas, cold gusty winters and unforgiving, peaty soil. But they are fundamentally similar, and – what's more – share some of the same birds.

Both heathland and moorland have arisen through the activities of our ancestors. Heathland was once a forest growing on acidic, well-drained soil, that was cleared and grazed and became overgrown with heather and gorse. This seems just about believable because, in many places, we can observe the encroachment of birch scrub or pine trees, and visualise the gradual disappearance of the low-level sward. But with moorland the transformation process is harder to imagine.

Somehow we have become so wedded to the idea of our northern uplands as ancient, barren and inhospitable that it seems almost sacrilege to think they were not always thus. In a few places, especially the boggiest parts, this may indeed be true. But most of our rugged moorland would eventually, given time and neglect, revert to a gentler landscape of prissy trees and shrubs, as it was before the tourists began to ogle it.

Neither of these habitats provides the warmest welcome for birds. Heather provides good cover, but it does not bring with it the richest invertebrate fauna; it's a bit like a Russian supermarket, plenty of the same but not much variety. So on heathland, many of the birds are drawn to patches of gorse instead, which is good for insects, and on moorland the inhabitants gravitate towards damp gullies, bogs and grassy swards. The acidic nature of the soil mitigates against a profusion of invading plants, and without this diversity there is little on the shelves to attract a wide variety of customers.

The two habitats are also somewhat lacking in vertical structure, with few layers of vegetation, which also counts against a good bird tally. Whilst scrub in its woodland edge guise offers tall patches, short patches and different forms of cover, much of this diversity is missing from heathland and moorland. With the lack of cover and shelter against the wind, any bird living here needs, at heart, to be an open country lover. Woodland wanderers need not apply.

Previous spread: A pair of Stonechats (male on left) on a spring heathland.

Below: Meadow Pipits quickly hit panic mode.

A male Hen Harrier quarters the moor in search of small birds and mammals.

If you visit a heathland or moorland in winter, you may be dismayed by the general lack of birds. It is perfectly possible to see almost nothing for hours on end – although you might hear the rattle of a Wren from somewhere deep in the heather; these versatile little birds get everywhere. But the key to heath watching is patience. Birds are here and they will show eventually. Some, indeed, are rare and special, but they don't give themselves up easily.

If you do break your duck, the bird you will probably first flush into sight will be a Meadow Pipit. This small, streaky brown insectivore is one of the few birds that is at home in long grass. It is primarily terrestrial, and walks around with something of an absent-minded look, as if it was searching for somewhere to have a picnic. Every so often it makes unconvincing pecks at the sward, completely without that purposeful air that most birds adopt when foraging. But when a Meadow Pipit is disturbed it goes straight into panic mode. It flutters up and blurts out a series of *sip*, *sip* calls, supposedly repeating its name, then begins to fly this way and that, hovering on the spot, turning, shifting, dithering, seeming unable to decide where to land and what to do. Clearly, this is not a bird for a crisis. It finally disappears with a dive, and presumably doesn't calm down for some time to come.

Meadow Pipits, though, despite their apparent inability to cope with life's surprises, are highly abundant on both heaths and moors. Tapping into the sward invertebrates without much competition, they are a dominant species of these landscapes. In turn, they form a vital part of the heathland and moorland food chains. Merlins and Hen Harriers, two predators of these habitats, take them in bushels, the former almost to the exclusion of everything else. Making up the lower building blocks of the heath economy, Meadow Pipits are a bit like the Epsilons in George Orwell's *Nineteen Eighty-Four*.

Quartering

Birds of prey are a major feature of moorland or heathland in winter, the openness of the habitat suiting them nicely. Indeed, both Merlins and Hen Harriers breed on British moors in summer and then often swap them for heaths in winter, sticking to a broad habitat type that they are used to and can comb efficiently for food.

The Hen Harrier – the larger of these two birds – has a special way of hunting known as quartering, which involves flying slowly just a few metres above the grass, bracken or heather and looking out for prey moving below. It can fly like this because it has a light body and large, long wings for buoyancy, and can use any zephyr of wind to keep it airborne, even at low speed.

Harriers probably acquire most of their food by flushing birds or mammals from cover, rather than actually taking them by surprise. And as we know, Meadow Pipits flush more easily and theatrically than most.

The Merlin, however, hunts in quite a different way. A compact raptor with broad-based but sharply pointed wings, it uses speed and surprise as its main tools for catching prey. It targets small birds, and generally flies low to the ground, hoping to surprise its prey by appearing suddenly from over the horizon and making a quick grab. But this pocket predator can sometimes also be much sneakier. On these occasions it won't try to conceal itself, but instead adopts an undulating flight pattern reminiscent of a thrush or some other harmless bird, and approaches the target flock as a wolf in sheep's clothing. Once its victims relax, the Merlin strikes.

Perch and pounce

With all this danger about, the small birds of the heath can pursue one of two survival strategies: either they can simply skulk in the heather all day, like a Wren; or they can venture out, but stay on guard. The essentially open nature of a heath or moor, remember, suits their enemies more than it suits them, so theirs must be a vigilance of the very highest order. Not many birds are up to this challenge.

One bird that is, though, is the Stonechat, an endearingly irritable mite, closely

related to the Robin. In common with that iconic garden bird, the Stonechat has a habit of sitting still on elevated perches, as though for our admiration, although it probably never actually sits on spades. It does this for a reason: its foraging technique is to scan the ground below in the hope of spying the movements of small insects, whereupon it can fly down and grab them. So it has large eyes for a small bird, and will quickly spot anything from an ant on the ground to an approaching Merlin. It keeps the whole of its territory under constant surveillance, like a feathered closed-circuit camera, and is usually well able to escape from most predators.

The Stonechat is so vigilant, in fact, that there exists a whole sub-culture of birds that use its abilities for their own protection. Perhaps they should be dubbed an underclass, because they tend to remain hidden in the foliage below a foraging Stonechat, feeding in peace but listening carefully for any *tsack* alarm call that might come from their "minder". And these birds do more than just exploit the Stonechat's vigilance when its territory overlaps with theirs: there is evidence that Wrens and Whitethroats, for instance, may actually follow the bolder birds around, using them as protection.

And it so happens that if you wish to see one of the most characteristic of all Britain's heathland birds, the once rare and threatened Dartford Warbler, you could do very much worse than to find a Stonechat first. For of all the guild of species that use security guards, the Dartford Warbler is the most persistent, frequent and well recorded. It has even been suggested that a kind of mutual benefit arises, in which the skulking Dartford Warbler flushes insects from the deep foliage and into the Stonechat's path, while the Stonechat keeps a general lookout for them both.

Heathland's signature bird, the Dartford Warbler.

Heather specialists

While most skulkers occur in heathland primarily because it offers dense, low cover and relatively few competitors, the Dartford Warbler has a much more intimate relationship with its habitat. It is the only British bird that breeds exclusively on heathland, and, furthermore, it occurs on heaths throughout the year – even sitting out chilly winters in what is already a tough habitat for survival. Something specific must be attracting it to this habitat, and the answer lies in the plants that make it up: namely, heather and gorse.

Detailed studies have confirmed the nature of the Dartford Warbler's dependence. Its nests are almost invariably in the heather, and at least half of these will be less than a metre above ground, where the growth is thickest. Some of the nest structure consists of heather itself. Meanwhile, most of the Dartford Warbler's foraging is done in nearby gorse bushes, this figure reaching a remarkable 87% in the springtime, when the birds start breeding. Clearly, a location without heather and gorse is hopeless for these attractive birds, and they deserve their status as the lowland heath's trademark species.

But there is one moorland bird that shows an even stronger dependence upon its habitat than that of the Dartford Warbler, with an even narrower compass. That bird is the Red Grouse, a bird whose ecology is so tangled up with heather that it is actually heather-coloured itself.

Red Grouse have a diet that, taken over a year, amounts to about 90% heather. They will nibble the green parts of other moorland plants if these are available, and berries when in season, but these extras are little more than seasoning for the main fare; without heather there are no Red Grouse. They also nest among the stuff, of course, and their chicks begin to eat the shoots when they are less than three weeks old (before that, it's invertebrates). So their dependence is complete. Strangely, the same species, where found abroad, has no such restrictions, and heather can form only a marginal part of the diet.

Now you might think that heather is heather, and that a Red Grouse on a heather moor has all that it needs. But you'd only be partly right. It turns out that some heather is better than other heather, just as some apples are tastier than other apples and – now we're on the subject – some whisky is finer than other whisky. Who knows whether the Grouse can taste the difference, but it turns out that heather growing on alkaline soil, as opposed to the more usual acid soil, is more nutritious; it is richer in protein and probably contains higher levels of essential minerals such as potassium. Thus the density of Red Grouse breeding on alkaline moors is greater and their nesting success is higher. Another subtle difference occurs between stands of heather: new shoots, for example, are more nutritious than older ones, yet the older ones provide better cover for nesting birds. All in all, there are enough refinements in Red Grouse ecology to keep the manager of a grouse moor gainfully occupied for years.

'What do I fancy today? I know – heather!'

Fringe benefits

The truly committed members of the heathland and moorland community are, however, in the minority, and it is surprising how many of the birds we think of as "core" heathland birds, such as Woodlarks or Nightjars, or "core" moorland birds, such as Curlews and Golden Plovers, are actually attracted by more marginal features. The Nightjar, for example, is attracted by the openness of the habitat, making it easy for this bird to forage in flight and to find a good spot for its eggs, but it does not require either heather or gorse as such. Similarly Golden Plovers and Curlews benefit from the invertebrate fauna of the bogs and pastures, rather than of the dry open moor itself. And the Tree Pipit is an even more marginal resident. It nests and feeds on the ground – benefiting, once again, from the combination of open areas and close nearby cover – but it will not cope without the presence of tall trees, such as pines or birches. This small bird is an inveterate show-off, and even though these trees serve only as singing perches, it will not colonise a heath without them. What a poser!

In fact, if you visit a moor or heath on a summer's day, and if you remain until darkness falls, you might get something of a false impression of this habitat. For a brief season it is quite rich in birds, and you might find yourself exaggerating its attractions to another bird-watcher. That's easy to do and easily forgiven, just as it is easy to think that the habitat has been here for all time.

"Here be dragons" – The Hobby's joy-ride

BIRD OF prey kills are usually private affairs. Somehow it seems unseemly to intrude upon their awful reality; the sight of the killer with talons locked in its victim can be unsettling, a scene that compels the viewer to look away for their own good. Attacks are also, as is so often the case with death, perfunctory and functional, without any frills. The Sparrowhawk strike is a case in point: a lightning swoop, a puff of feathers, and then it's all over. The adrenalin doesn't last long. Only the avian spectators make a fuss, and even their clamour soon passes.

So we seldom see birds of prey at work. A celebrated Scottish ornithologist, for example, who walked the Highlands for twenty years, only twice saw a Golden Eagle strike in all that time. And Goshawks are equally discreet, so much so that we can only assess their feeding habits by waiting to see what they bring to the nest. We may even struggle to see a Buzzard dive upon its favourite rodent food, or catch a Merlin locking on to the course of a Skylark, driving it to exhaustion with the persistence of a guided missile. Such events generally take place far from our prying eyes.

But the Hobby is different. This streamlined falcon only comes to visit us for the warm summer months, occurring rather sparingly over heath and farmland. Unusually for a raptor, its hunting arena is up high in the open air, so when it is marauding, you cannot really miss it. This makes its killings – compared with those of other birds of prey – highly public affairs.

But in mitigation, the dashing chases of the Hobby have a spontaneity and grace that some-what redeems their murderous nature. This bird works the most difficult habitat for taking prey by surprise: uncluttered airspace. So it must rely upon supreme flying skill to set upon its prey, rather than upon pure stalking. The Hobby is very quick, very manoeuvrable and, with its neat, slim form, cuts a real dash in the sky. So thrilling and elegant are its catches, and so very watchable, that we forget they are kills, and that their results are as final as the sad wrecks on a Sparrowhawk plucking post. Somehow the deaths are almost stylish. If a Hobby were a human killer,

it would surely be James Bond.

The Hobby's prey varies according to the season, but when this hunter first arrives from Africa, in the middle of May, it goes primarily for what might seem to be odd fare for a raptor – insects. It is difficult to imagine how these diminutive and hard-bodied creatures might sustain a bird of this size, but then the Hobby doesn't just go for routine insects; it goes for the big and fast ones. Dragonflies are a great favourite, because they often fly higher than the rest, motoring about the skies with the same brash confidence that every predator has. And they make a reasonable snack. To catch them, the Hobby usually swoops low over a heathland pond or bog, and then makes a quick upward turn to snatch the insect from below, using its feet. This isn't as straight-forward as it might sound: dragonflies are quick and nimble flyers, with sharp eyes. The snatch must be perfected by practice. And the birds often miss. But if you are watching one in action, you can always tell when a strike has been success-ful, because the bird feeds in midair, nonchalantly keeping steady as it clutches the victim in its talons and dismantles the

A Hobby finally homes in on a juvenile Swallow after a long chase.

Not many birds of prey are fast enough to catch large dragonflies.

exoskeleton with its bill.

One strategy that often yields high returns for a Hobby is to hunt in the evening, when the insects may be swarming and thinking more about mating than evading capture. In common with many birds of prey, the Hobby sees very acutely in low lighting conditions, and using the same trick of coming from below as it does with dragonflies, and thereby silhouetting them against the bright sky, it can pick off good numbers of moths or beetles in a short bout of feasting. There are plenty of large, turbo-charged moths on heathland, and equal numbers of slow, lumbering beetles. (Have you ever been struck by a May Bug? Me, too). So the Hobby often goes to roost on a full stomach. Later on in the season, however, when youngsters are in the nest and pleading for food, a parent Hobby needs to seek somewhat

more substantial fare than insects. So it turns to birds instead. In fact the timing is perfect: Hobbies lay their eggs when summer is well advanced, with the express purpose of picking off the hordes of inexperienced juvenile birds that are taking uncertainly to the skies at that time. Conveniently, though, there are also more hefty insects about then than at other times of year, and the main provider, the male, can keep itself fed by picking these off whilst out hunting birds.

You might not think that juvenile birds would be any easier to catch than their parents; after all, they don't wear their forlorn, unprepared-for-life look for very long once out of the nest, but are soon lean and quick. But we are talking about very small parameters here. In top level sport, if you're not totally on your game, you lose. In the same way, inexperienced birds are probably just fractionally less flight-efficient and worldly than their parents, but this fraction is all a hunter needs, and the youngsters are ruthlessly picked off.

The sorts of birds that Hobbies hunt are open-country creatures such as larks, pipits, Swallows and martins. It requires sublime flying skills to catch these quintessentially moving targets, especially since Swallows and martins are every bit as aerial as their nemesis. Yet the Hobby does have one trick that these birds cannot match, and that is acceleration. If it rises high above its intended quarry, it can then use wing-beats and gravity to reach dizzying speeds in a manoeuvre known as a "stoop", which is essentially a long targeted dive. Several birds of prey perform stoops, but the Hobby is more manoeuvrable than most, and can cope with the most extreme evasive measures from its intended victim.

On occasion, remarkably, the Hobby can even catch Swifts. These birds are the ultimate aerial performers, and few hunters would lift a wing to challenge them. But Hobbies do, and their own streamlined shape, with its slim body and narrow, swept-back wings, even mirrors that of this most awkward of targets. Swifts are certainly not standard fare, and usually constitute only a tenth or so of a Hobby's diet; but the fact that they feature at all is testimony to this aerial killer's remarkable potency. To see a Hobby catch a Swift – and I myself have witnessed it – is just too awe-inspiring ever to seem unpleasant or voyeuristic.

How do you want your Swift, sir – shaken or stirred?

The night-swallow

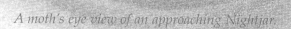

IF YOU'VE ever been
birdwatching on a
heathland by night, you'll
be aware to your cost that this
habitat
contains plenty of nocturnal insects.
In fact, on a warm evening there may
be clouds of the pesky things, and it
seems that you cannot walk more than a
few paces before being bitten by an
unseen midge or struck by some moth or
beetle that was hurrying past without
looking, like a preoccupied commuter
dashing for a bus. For a human being
these insects are something of an
annoyance, yet for birds they constitute
an almost limitless aerial buffet. There
are literally thousands of tiny bodies out
there, just waiting to be eaten.

But it isn't quite that simple. Insects are
very hard to hunt at night. Most are
exceedingly small, many are highly mobile,
and their movements are, of course, cloaked
in darkness. The difficulties of this sort of night
foraging are, for most, insurmountable.

One species of heathland bird, however,
manages to thrive on it. This is the Nightjar, a
Kestrel-sized bird with camouflaged plumage, a
large head and remarkably small legs. A battery of
adaptations enables it to exploit its demanding
diet, and its strange appearance and nocturnal
habits have made it the subject of all sorts of
peculiar folklore. It was once known as the
"goatsucker", for example, because it was
believed to drink the milk from the teats of these
domestic animals at night. The Nightjar is a
summer migrant to Britain, here only in the
warmest months when there is plenty of insect life
around. In early autumn it departs for tropical
Africa where, not surprisingly, it carries on hunting nocturnal insects as it did here. And, funnily
enough, there are plenty of goats in Africa, too.

Although the Nightjar, of course, does not milk
goats, a good look at its highly unusual mouth
helps explain some of the wild stories that have
circulated about the way it feeds. The bill looks

A moth's eye view of an approaching Nightjar.

relatively tiny and harmless, but you'll get quite a
shock if you ever catch a Nightjar yawning at you,
because its gape is both enormously capacious
and gaudy pink, recalling the open jaws of a
snake in mid-strike. In fact, the opening of its
enormous mouth is one of the Nightjar's defence
mechanisms, and it can also hiss at the same time
and thus put on quite a horror show to a potential
predator. This gape, though, is actually an extreme
adaptation for catching insects in flight. Most
unusually, the Nightjar's jaw does not just open
up and down but also moves from side to side,
allowing the bird some lateral movement in case
an insect tries to escape the advancing bird to the
left or right. The mouth, therefore, functions
rather like a butterfly net, with plenty of volume
for engulfing insects efficiently.

Its lateral jaw movement is not the only
unusual feature of a Nightjar's mouth. The palate
is also highly sensitive, which means that an
insect hitting its surface sends an immediate

signal to snap the bill shut. This sounds ponderous in words, but in reality the reaction is lightning fast, and the prey is enveloped almost instantaneously. And it needs to be fast: larger insects might bounce off the Nightjar's palate and escape if they weren't entrapped immediately, especially given the momentum of their collision.

Yet another adaptation for insect capture is found around the edge of the Nightjar's mouth, in the form of bristles – which are in fact highly modified feathers. These are attached to special muscles, allowing them a measure of independent movement. Essentially, they form a "hairy" ring to the mouth, as if the Nightjar had neglected to shave for a few weeks, and they doubtless help to channel insects in from the margins. Recent experiments suggest that these bristles may also play a tactile role, detecting food in the same way as the palate. But whatever function they perform, they are clearly highly important, because they form a vital part of the Nightjar's grooming routine. The claw on a Nightjar's middle toe is fitted with tiny indentations, making it a little like a comb and – surprise, surprise – the Nightjar spends much time running its bristles lovingly through this claw. Well, we all need a little grooming now and then.

Thus far, you might have concluded that the Nightjar is, in effect, a flying net that trawls indiscriminately through the clouds of heathland insects. Well, the bird almost certainly does obtain some smaller food such as mosquitoes and midges in this way, but the larger and more nutritious morsels are simply not distributed densely enough in the night sky to make this an efficient strategy. So the Nightjar is more selective. The truth is, it is a hunter like any other, and the procurement of the most satisfying food is a question of finding, chasing and catching.

So, even though it usually hunts in the darkness, the Nightjar locates most of its prey by sight.

To this end, it shows a number of adaptations. First, and in common with most nocturnal birds and mammals, it has large eyes for its size. So large, in fact, that the nostrils have been moved out of the way – so to speak – behind the mandibles. Second, the light-detecting cells in the retina contain fewer oil droplets than those of most other birds, and this is thought to be an adaptation to enhance the detection of contrast, as opposed to colour, in the night sky. And the third adaptation is the most unusual because, uniquely among birds, Nightjars have a tapetum. This is a little like a mirror set behind the retina; it reflects any light that has passed by the photoreceptor cells right back through them, to ensure that as much light as possible is registered. Cats and other nocturnal mammals also have a tapetum, which is why their eyes seem to glow in the dark. If you took a torch to a Nightjar (but please don't, it's illegal), its eyes would do the same.

Thus, the Nightjar flies through the darkness using its exceptionally acute vision to find food. It tends to be most active just after dusk and before dawn, and also when the moon is bright, when it has the best opportunity to see prey; in complete darkness it will either rest or make short sallying flights from a perch in the manner of a flycatcher. And, of course, it is also highly adapted for manoeuvrable flight, its long, pointed wings and relatively small body giving it buoyancy and agility in the air. It can jink, accelerate or hover, according to need.

All in all, the Nightjar is one of Britain's most highly adapted species. It hawks just like a Swallow and, in a way, takes the night-time shift vacated by that better known bird.

In inclement weather Nightjars often sit on branches and make short darting sallies to catch what they spot.

Songs from the heights

In common with many species of birds, the Curlew has dull plumage but a great voice.

MOORLAND DOESN'T have a great many fans. True, it can be a dreary habitat to look at, except perhaps in the late summer and autumn when the heather turns the landscape stunningly purple. And it can be lonely, too, and windswept, and inhospitable. But those same people to whom moorland is bore-land should try visiting on a calm spring morning, when the sun rises without hindrance from cloud. Then, if they choose the right places, they might just see and hear one of the finest avian shows in Britain; an aerial performance of such extraordinary choreography, set to an accompaniment of sounds so wild and exultant, that the visitor is – for one vivid moment – completely transfixed by the experience. They may never think of moorland in quite the same way again.

Four different wading birds are responsible for this miracle: the Snipe, the Curlew, the Golden Plover and the Lapwing. It would be easy enough to run through their routines step by step, and describe their breeding displays in meticulous detail, but that wouldn't capture any of the magic of the scene. So instead, let's take a flight of fancy. Imagine for a moment that we are standing in the right spot, in the right conditions, at the right time of year; and all around us the open moorland is still lit by nothing more than a pre-dawn glow. Let the show begin.

The first act, like an overture, plays only to the ears. From out of the darkness comes a gentle throbbing sound, a little like the distant bleating of a sheep. This eerie noise comes and goes,

as though at the mercy of non-existent gusts of wind. At one moment it seems to be approaching, and you realise how mechanical it is, almost like that irritating noise that model aircraft make. But, just as quickly, it fades again into the silence.

As you ponder this mystery, a whistle of extraordinary clarity breaks from the same patch of sky. Or rather, it is two whistles: a single introductory note followed by a double note slurring down in pitch. Together their effect is like a pitiful sigh of almost unbearable sadness. This is the song of the Golden Plover, and its voice seems to emanate so perfectly from the clear air of its surroundings that you cannot help but feel it tug at your emotions.

The melancholy mood is soon banished by loud, exultant, laughing tones. A dominant sound of the moor, the Curlew's song is more than just a few high notes or a distant buzzing. Instead, this is a full-on phrase, with a startling beginning and a sensational finish. It sets off as a series of quavering whistles, and these crescendo, with the notes almost tripping over each other, until they merge

In flight display, the madcap Lapwing throws itself about, up and down and side to side.

into one long, ecstatic bubbling trill. As this phrase ceases, the moor falls briefly silent, as though the Curlew is waiting for applause. But it never comes.

Instead another noise breaks the silence. This is neither sad nor joyful, but different still. It has something of the insane about it, with wild whoops and yodels, and a curious noise that can only be likened to the sound of tearing sellotape from its roll. Of the four waders, this manic yelping of the Lapwing can be the most persistent noise of all, rolling on and on, as if some alcohol-fuelled party were being held out here in the wilderness. And this joyful madness delights you before you even see the birds responsible for the performance zooming across the sky.

And zoom they do – especially the author of our bleating sound, the Snipe. This bird's song-flight takes it on something of a roller-coaster ride: it sets off flying in a gentle curve, powered by very fast wing-beats and gradually rising in height until, at about 50 metres up, it suddenly dives down almost to ground level, only to fly upwards again, still keeping its circular path as though tethered on a long string, before plummeting once more. It is during these rapid descents that the strange mechanical throbbing noise is made. Amazingly, it is not created by the bird's vocal apparatus, but by its feathers. Special muscle attachments on the outermost feathers of a Snipe's tail enable it to move these feathers apart from the others, causing them to vibrate in the wind and produce the unusual noise that is traditionally called "drumming". This signal is audible a long way away, and thus enhances the bird's display routine – presumably saving it some vital energy.

It's not always easy to see a Snipe drumming but, in our imaginary dawn, we can just about catch a glimpse of it dashing past, long bill pointing down and wings beating with robotic evenness and frightening speed, before it disappears into the loam. But the Curlew is a much more visible performer. For a start it is a much larger bird. And its display is slower-paced than the high-speed Snipe's, too. So we can watch the Curlew easily as it takes off, flies on full wing-beats up to a moderate height, hovers briefly and then glides down on stiff, slightly raised wings, bubbling as it goes. It might then fly up again and glide down a second time, always following a straight course, like a giant Woodpigeon. That's enough, though. As it settles on the ground, the Curlew gives a quick lift of the wings, like a victorious Olympic athlete acknowledging the crowd.

Only when the sun has risen might we catch sight of the displaying Golden Plover. High above us the glint of white underwings reveals a bird that we could not previously see. And that's the idea. The Golden Plover doesn't have a complex song or an elaborate display, but it does have these flashing white underwings, an advertisement of its existence that needs little embellishment. So it just flies around, sometimes up to a mind-blowing 300 metres, wailing its song and flapping those wings with a slow, exaggerated upstroke, visible from miles around.

It's up to the Lapwing to produce the really intricate stuff, and indeed its flight-display is so complicated that, were it an Olympic sport, even ice-dance judges might be left scratching their heads in bewilderment. But we're not here to adjudicate: we've just come to enjoy the show. The Lapwing's display suits its madcap song perfectly. The bird flies up and down, twists and turns, rocks its body back and forth as though buffeted by heavy waves, and tumbles down seemingly out of control. Everything about it is reckless and uninhibited, free and wild.

And as we watch and listen to these aerial acrobats in full flow, the mood is catching, and we return to our lives slightly less weighed down, and just a little inspired.

FARMLAND

Fields of change

MOST OF us love the British countryside with a passion, but we sometimes have trouble defining what exactly it is that we like. Indeed, our love is probably infatuation: we adore what we see, but cannot quite deal with what lies behind the facade. Our imaginations preserve a romanticised ideal of farmland; a pastoral idyll where children roam safe and free, and where the perpetually sunny fields brim with all kinds of life – especially birds. But this is not the reality, and our love must accommodate the fact that the here and now of farmland is very different indeed.

FARMLAND, IN fact, is a troubled habitat. Those working the soil are leaving the profession in droves, disillusioned by bureaucracy and squeezed financially from all sides. They follow in the footsteps of their birds, which have been declining at even faster rates than farmers' profits for at least the last forty years. So, while more than 60% of our land is farmed in some way and may still look green and pleasant, it is quietly being evacuated. Some farmland birds have even fled to gardens, where the landscape is hardly natural but where the welcome is warmer.

A strict definition of farmland would identify it as any kind of land used for the commercial production of biological resources, and this would include orchards and forestry and the like. However, in the eyes of most people there are only two main types of farming: arable farming, which produces crops, and pastoral farming, which raises live animals. In terms of their birdlife these two types of farming share a good many species, and many farms practise both systems.

Above: Farmland fields can provide rich pickings for Rooks and Jackdaws.

Previous spread: An arable scene, with Pheasant, Swallow and Chaffinch.

However, there are some differences between the two styles which are reflected in their birds.

Pastoral farmland

Sheep, cows and horses, Britain's livestock stalwarts, all conveniently eat grass, so most pastoral fields are simply wide open grassy swards. A livestock farmer's efforts are directed more to the welfare of the animals than to the fields themselves, which tends to mean that this habitat changes less during the year, and from one year to another, than does arable farmland. Of the three grazing tenants, sheep are the most voracious, cutting the grass shorter than the others and creating a more uniform effect. Cow-grazed fields will probably have a greater variety of grass length. But, on the whole, similar birds coexist on all three.

The birds you are mostly likely to see first when you scan pastoral fields are members of the crow family. In sheep country, Carrion or Hooded Crows can be everywhere. These and Ravens feed off the carcasses of dead lambs and other casualties, as well as taking a wide variety of other food items. Rooks, too, feed on pastoral fields in large flocks, probing the earth for worms and leatherjackets, while on their coat-tails their smaller relatives, Jackdaws, pick items from the surface. In the summer Jackdaws abound in longer grass, snatching small moths and other surface-living insects to feed to their young.

Another mainstay of pastoral fields is the bustling Starling. Although we tend to think of Starlings as birds of town and city, they are actually specialist feeders on open grassland and are often abundant on farmland fields. Their bill is adapted for probing in the soil, with the muscle for opening it being stronger than the one for closing it. They insert this bill into a soft substrate, open it to create a small hole, and then peer into the hole for signs of food, using excellent low-light vision that is adapted for just this sort of dark nook or cranny. Although Starlings breed on farmland, they are usually more abundant on fields during winter, when their ranks are swelled with visitors from the continent.

The grassland sward often holds a high mammal population, and this ensures good hunting for predators such as Kestrels and Barn Owls. Studies have recently revealed that Kestrels select their feeding territories on the basis of vole density, which of course makes perfect sense. Remarkably, though, they are able to gauge this density by observing the network of urine trails that the voles leave on the surface. In common with Starlings, Kestrels have special vision for their work: the trails

only show up in the ultraviolet spectrum.

Pastoral land, with its wide-open aspect, can also offer ideal conditions for both breeding and wintering waders. In northern England and Scotland, such birds as Oystercatcher, Lapwing and Curlew will all nest in rough patches of farmland, especially in damp areas, and in winter the Lapwing and the Golden Plover occur widely on fields of all kinds. These latter two are both sight-feeders that rely on subtle clues to pick earthworms and other invertebrate prey from the soil, so they tend to favour short swards.

Arable farmland

Arable farmland, by its very nature, is forever slave to the activities required to make a profit from it. Crops must be sown, grown and harvested. They are usually fertilised, and protected against unwanted competition in the form of weeds and plant-eating invertebrates. Not surprisingly, every farmland bird's fortunes are also determined by this yearly cycle of crop husbandry, for better or for worse. In no other habitat is the bird population so closely bound up with commercial human activity.

Contrary to what many countryside-lovers might imagine, standing crop fields often make poor habitats for birds because there is so little diversity in the vegetation, both among the species present (mono-cultures prevail) and in their physical properties – the stems are close-set, for example, and there are often no branches. Nevertheless, a few birds do breed among crops of various sorts. The Skylark is one of the most common and widespread. A small ground-nesting species, it places its cup among short growing stems, almost in the open. The ground is a dangerous place to bring up your young and, to cope with the perils the Skylark has one of the shortest incubation periods of any bird in the world – as little as 11 days. Another species closely associated

Corn Buntings may carry on singing even throughout long summer days.

23

with the crops themselves is the Corn Bunting. In contrast to the Skylark, the Corn Bunting usually nests in tall, well-grown fields, especially of cereals such as barley, but again, the nest is usually placed on the ground. The Corn Bunting's way of quickly removing its brood from the dangerously accessible nest is not to shorten the incubation period, but to lead the young away before they can actually fly – as early as nine days after they are born. This behaviour is common in birds such as ducks and waders, but highly unusual in songbirds such as buntings.

Both the Skylark and the Corn Bunting provide a highly distinctive soundtrack to the arable environment. The Skylark's exultant aerial song hardly needs introduction, but the Corn Bunting's ditty – a dry jingle like the shaking of a set of keys – is now seldom heard, so badly has this species been affected by modern farming practices. The male Corn Bunting has a habit of singing all day virtually throughout the breeding season. Its indefatigable effort has an ulterior motive, because the Corn Bunting will continuously attempt to attract new mates throughout the long breeding summer. One fecund male Corn Bunting was once reported to have acquired 18 mates in a single season, a British record for polygamy.

Midnight callers

Two rarities in Britain nest mainly among arable crops. One is the Stone-curlew, a strange bird related to the waders, which hunts for insects on short swards at night; another is the equally odd and nocturnal Corncrake, which keeps its head down in the long grass. They occur at opposite ends of the country, the Stone-curlew on chalk downland in Central and Southern England, and the Corncrake in Scotland and Ireland. The latter is an arable bird by dint of occurring mostly in fields grown for hay.

A third, more widespread arable species is the Quail, which occurs in still taller vegetation than the Corncrake, often among crops such as barley or wheat, where it is virtually impossible to see. This is yet another species that seems to be most active in twilight, or when it is dark.

All of these birds were once much more widespread in Britain than now, and where they occurred together they must have made night-time eerily atmospheric. Each has a loud voice that carries well in the darkness: the Stone-curlew makes wailing and whistling sounds; the Quail gives a soft, rhythmic "wet-me-lips"; and the Corncrake punctuates the air with a loud rasping "crex, crex", from which it derives its scientific name. All of these sounds have

ventriloquial properties, so in days gone by the lonely farm worker walking home in the dark might easily have felt himself surrounded and pursued by mysterious voices, and perhaps quickened his step.

Quail, Corncrake and Stone-curlew also share the migratory habit, being summer visitors to Britain that arrive in spring and depart in autumn. Quails have a particularly unusual migration, sometimes showing the peculiar habit of arriving here in force very late in the season, in July or even August. Scientists have recently discovered that these latecomers are birds that reached North Africa from the Tropics in the early spring, bred there and then travelled north with their new generation to breed again – a strategy followed by a few butterflies, but no other European bird.

The weird Stone Curlew is most active in twilight.

Farmland borders

There is, of course, a great deal more to farmland than just fields. Farmland is set in a mosaic of its own making, the open country dotted by settlements and pockets of woodland. On a smaller scale, the commercial nature of agriculture ensures that areas owned by different people must be delineated in some way, be it with a fence, a wall, a hedgerow, a bank or a ditch, and on the whole these boundaries have proved hugely beneficial to birds. Ditches, for example, especially if filled with water, may provide nest-sites for such species as Sedge Warblers, Reed Buntings and Moorhens. Dry-stone walls play host to Wheatears and other hole-nesters.

The most celebrated border features are, of course, hedgerows. The Enclosure Acts of 1750 and beyond were surely among the most beneficial laws for birds ever passed in Britain, since they and the informal agreements that pre-dated them led to the creation of thousands of miles of hedgerows – a few of which, planted at that time, even still exist today.

Hedgerows can be good bird habitats in their

own right, harbouring various breeding species, but just as importantly they can also act as carriageways between woods. Birds passing through can grab a bite to eat, much as people on the move refuel at service stations. Older hedgerows tend to be the best, not only because they are often larger than younger counterparts, but also because they are richer in their ecology. There is a direct correlation between the age of a hedgerow and its plant diversity. Not surprisingly, an enhanced diversity supports a wondrously rich invertebrate fauna which, in turn, attracts many birds.

A good many hedgerow birds are primarily woodland inhabitants that have spilled over into this habitat and found it to their liking. These include such familiar faces as Song Thrushes, Dunnocks, Blackbirds, Chaffinches and Wrens. Others are typical of more scrubby habitats, including Whitethroats and Linnets. A few, though, can also be thought of as hedgerow specialists and, of these, the best known must be the Yellowhammer. More of these buttery-yellow birds live along our hedgerows than in any other habitat. The territorial males divide a hedgerow linearly between them, with each bird owning an average of 60 metres, and each rattles out his famous "little bit of bread and no cheese" ditty up to 7,000 times a day.

Another species with strong hedgerow connections is the Grey Partridge. It doesn't occur in the midst of the hedgerow proper, but nests at its foot in the undergrowth along the field border. Here it lays the largest clutch of any British bird, and possibly any species anywhere: an average of 15 eggs. The female is a very tight sitter, which is hardly surprising, given the size of the brood she has to protect and incubate. The Grey Partridge is also one of our most terrestrial birds, spending almost all of its life on the ground and being highly reluctant to take flight. It lives in

small family parties, known as coveys, whose members patrol the area encompassed by just a few fields for their entire lives. You could say that its horizons are rather limited.

Trouble on the farm

You might visit farmland on a regular basis, but how often have you actually seen a Grey Partridge? The chances are, hardly ever; possibly even never. This is now a scarce bird. It's all the more remarkable, then, that just a couple of hundred years ago the Grey Partridge was one of the commonest birds in the whole of Britain. Even in the 1950s it was a familiar sight to everyone who lived on the land below the mountains, and many people alive today will remember when the sight of one would not have caused a murmur. Yet from 1967–1999, Grey Partridge numbers in England are estimated to have declined by a whopping 86%. It is quite possible that nothing will halt this trend, and that the bird will disappear from Britain completely within a lifetime.

Sadly, this story is not confined to the Grey Partridge. Other farmland species have also suffered huge declines in the same period: Corn Bunting populations are down 85%, Turtle Doves 81%, Yellowhammers 39% and Lapwings 37%, and all over a massive area. Clearly, something is wrong down on the farm.

The unfortunate truth is that modern farming does not suit birds. A whole suite of changes have been introduced in the last fifty years to make farming more cost-effective, and these in combination have tended to produce an agriculture landscape that is a veritable ecological desert for birds and other wildlife. A closer look at some of these changes can illustrate the difficulties.

Change for the worse

Perhaps the most obvious change to our farming practices has been the increase in mechanisation, which enables a wider area of field to be

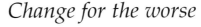

An iconic bird of farmland hedgerows, the Yellowhammer has suffered a steep decline in numbers.

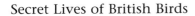

harvested more quickly and efficiently than ever before. As a result, there is less spillage available for birds, both on the field itself and around the storehouses. Farming is simply a less messy business than it used to be. And with quick coverage of a field now much easier, farmers have been quick to remove boundaries and other unwanted features, such as ponds or patches of scrub, that get in the way of the machines and reduce the amount of profitable land. This wipes out large areas of habitat for such birds as Reed Buntings, Grey Partridges, Yellowhammers and Whitethroats.

The second most important development as far as birds are concerned has been the development of agrochemicals (in tandem with more efficient machines to spread them). Herbicides wipe out weeds and pesticides reduce the invertebrate fauna, and the effect this has had on birds has been little short of catastrophic. Thus, for instance, Grey Partridge and Corn Bunting chicks do not have enough insects to feed upon, and Turtle Dove have too few weed seeds to sustain them. Fertilisers also increase the density of some crops, making them grow too fast and tall to suit Skylarks and Lapwings during the breeding season.

A less known, but exceedingly important change has been the timing of tilling. There has been a widespread switch from sowing in the spring, to sowing in the autumn and growing winter wheat. Although this might not seem disastrous, the practice has effectively banished winter stubbles from our fields. Stubbles have historically been superb feeding sites for all our seed-eating farmland birds, including Skylarks, Yellowhammers, Corn Buntings, sparrows and finches, and their loss has been a significant factor in the decline of all these species. Even the House Sparrow has been a victim of this change, and the fall in the farmland population of these birds may have had a knock-on effect on urban and suburban populations, which in some places have suffered almost catastrophic losses.

There are, in fact, a bewildering number of factors that have altered the suitability of various types of farmland for birds. Increased stocking rates on pastoral farmland, for example, have affected breeding Lapwings, Stone-curlews and other ground-nesting birds, because the higher number of animals means that nests are more liable to be trampled. The Corncrake and Quail have been adversely affected by the general shift away from haymaking towards silage production, because this involves mowing the grass earlier in the season, which is lethal to their chicks.

Changes in modern farming have brought the odd benefit to some birds. The increased popularity of oilseed rape, for example, has provided opportunities for Linnets, Reed Buntings and Woodpigeons, while the introduction of set-aside schemes could yet save many of our species, albeit perhaps only in pockets. Set-aside was a quirky system introduced in 1992 to reduce the European Union's arable crop surpluses. Farmers were obliged to 'set aside' chunks of their land from production in order to receive certain financial benefits. In other words, farmers were paid to leave some of their land alone, which – theoretically, at least – would benefit birds and other wildlife. The system hasn't always been as beneficial as it might have been: some schemes have, for example, allowed spraying and mowing at inconvenient times for wildlife. But that does not mean that these problems cannot be overcome in the future.

Overall, though, the modernisation of farming has been hard for birds to handle, with the future not looking particularly rosy. And this makes us reflect on the past. Our romantic ideal of farmland is certainly no more than fantasy in these days of monoculture and autumn sowing. Yet perhaps, when we understand how our farmland once teemed with birdlife, we can see that this fantasy was once a reality. Today, sadly, that reality is long gone.

The fad for planting oilseed rape means that the future is rosier for the Linnet.

Whispering death

IT FLOATS in the air with the grace of wind-blown gossamer, and its soft white plumage gleams ethereally in evening sunshine or car headlights, but the Barn Owl's undeniable charisma belies the truth – that it is an incorrigible killer. The truth about this bird is far from our storybook notion of a wise old owl. It might look wise, but its brain is so absorbed in a network of sensory information processing that it is closer to a hunting machine than a thinking being. And though it might appear cuddly and friendly, with those soft feathers removed the Barn Owl would be all deadly bill and talons: a predator, not a plaything.

But as a consummate killer of rodents and other prey, the Barn Owl is at least merciful – albeit unintentionally. If you have to die, then it's surely better to go quickly and in blissful ignorance of your fate. And that is invariably what happens to the Barn Owl's prey: death swoops in unannounced, with barely a whisper and with complete finality. That, in a way, is a form of mercy.

There is probably no other avian hunter that can approach its prey as silently as an owl can. One imagines that a Sparrowhawk's swoop or a Kestrel's plunge must at least make some kind of "*swoosh*", and that the victim must endure a tiny agonising instant in which it hears death coming. An approaching owl, though, makes not a sound. Its wings are modified in several ways to reduce noise: the primary feathers on the leading edge have a comb-like fringe that streamlines the air upward over the wing in flight; the feathers making up the trailing edge also have a hair-like fringe to dull the sound of turbulence; and all the flight feathers have a downy surface that dampens the sound they make when brushing together. These adaptations combine to make the owl a virtually silent flyer.

A Barn Owl also has very large wings for its size and a light body to lift. This contributes to the silence of its flight, making the bird unusually buoyant and thus able to stay aloft with minimum effort. The combination of large wings and lightness lends the Barn Owl's flight a jinking, almost acrobatic style, in which it can easily make quick turns, swoops and dives. Barn Owls have been observed doubling back on themselves and almost somersaulting on to prey that they detected when

almost past it. Theirs is the ideal flight for a predator that quarters slowly at a height of about 3m: low enough to scour the ground; high enough to scan a wide area.

However specialised its flight might be, though, there is one factor above all others that enables the Barn Owl to fly with stealth towards its prey: it hunts mostly at night. Small mammals feeding in the darkness cannot see their nemesis approaching, never mind hear it, and thus none of their senses can warn them of the approaching danger. For any predator that can use it, darkness is a great friend.

Although owls are celebrated for having large eyes and good nocturnal vision, the Barn Owl is less well endowed than most; its eyes, in fact, are relatively small. Instead it has what is possibly among the most accurate directional hearing of any animal in the world, and it is this that helps it to work at night and even, at times, in complete darkness. In experiments carried out in blackened buildings, where no light whatsoever could penetrate, scientists discovered that Barn Owls could catch mice entirely by ear. Better than that, they could pinpoint minute sounds in total darkness to an accuracy of a couple of degrees, both in the horizontal and vertical plane.

This extraordinary ability arises, once again, from a battery of adaptations. One of the most obvious adaptation is the Barn Owl's peculiar heart-shaped face. With the ears placed on the edge of skull, the two facial discs – made up from dense feathers – actually aim reflected sound towards the ears, thereby both directing the noise and amplifying it as it goes. As a further adaptation the ears are large and, of course, highly sensitive – especially to the

A Barn Owl takes a break. In contrast to other owls, it has a heart-shaped face and small, black eyes.

A Barn Owl detects prey . . . takes aim . . . and strikes with a downward lunge, feet first.

high-pitched noises made by rustling or squeaking rodents.

It is the orientation of the ears, though, that gives the Barn Owl its complete mastery of the night air's soundscape, and enables it to pinpoint prey with such accuracy. First, the ears are set well apart on the side of the Barn Owl's comparatively wide skull. This ensures that, when a sound arrives in the horizontal plane, it reaches one ear a fraction of a second before the other, and also registers more loudly on the side from which the sound is emanating. The time lapse is minute, but it is enough to give away the direction of the sound. We use exactly this technique for our own noise detection, but what is remarkable about the Barn Owl is that its ears are just as sensitive in the vertical plane, and that's because their openings are not symmetrical. In a Barn Owl, the left ear is higher up the skull than the right ear. Thus the same time-lapse gives directional information in the vertical plane, too. Truly, the Barn Owl has a three-dimensional sense of hearing.

As we wonder at this remarkable adaptation, those other bodily modifications to silent flight also fit neatly into the equation. For the Barn Owl doesn't just depend on its own silence for sneaking up upon prey, it also depends upon ambient silence for its ears to work at their best. If its wings whooshed, the sound could drown out the tiny stirrings of a mouse or vole. Silent wings make for attentive ears.

None of this is any consolation for a rodent, which simply needs to keep quiet. At the merest whisper, death arrives. Silently.

Ups and downs in the lives of larks

FOR A bird that is supposed to be a citizen of the air, and even gets its name from its aerial outpourings, the Skylark certainly spends a lot of time on the ground. In fact, when it gathers in flocks at the end of autumn and spends its time picking grain from fields, it disappears from many people's consciousness altogether and some even conclude that it must be a summer visitor, like a Swallow. But the Skylark isn't a summer visitor, and its engaging song-flight, so redolent of fair weather, is only one part of its overall behaviour. Its real life is led on the soil, where its brown plumage hides it from danger, and where all its fortunes, good or bad, are ultimately decided.

One popular idea about the Skylark is certainly true, though: it is certainly a farmland bird. It does frequent other habitats, especially moorland

The brown, streaky Skylark isn't much to look at on the ground…

. . . but becomes a star performer in the air.

and coastal dunes, but the bulk of the population resides where the bird's folklore arises – on Britain's arable fields. The legend of the Skylark, the bird that has sung its way exultantly into English literature and music, is at least grounded in reality, which is more than can be said for our perceptions of many other birds. (Owls? Wise? Are you joking?)

We wouldn't notice Skylarks at all, of course, if they didn't sing. And yet, if you really listen, the song itself isn't particularly special. It's far too shrill for many ears, and although there is variety in the articulation of its phrases, the overall pitch does not alter much. If you had to listen to a Skylark all day, at least with the intensity that you might bring to a concert, you would probably find the experience uncomfortable after a while.

However, you cannot fault the Skylark for style. It does sometimes sing from the ground or a low post, but more usually it takes to the air and, by doing so, makes sure that its message is transmitted in every direction and for some distance. The performance is a choreographed routine as well as a song. The bird rises in a hover, singing lustily. The ascent follows a slow, spiralling course until, at 50m or so above ground, it levels out. Almost invisible in the bright sky, the lark continues to perform, and as it does so its song seems to pour down in torrents, drenching the landscape below. The performance draws to a close as the bird once

again spirals down, and then, seemingly without warning, shuts off its recital, folds its wings and plummets back to earth.

You might think that all this palaver would take quite a while to complete, but surprisingly, the average length of a Skylark's complete performance has been measured at anything from two to two-and-a-half minutes – not even the length of a pop song. To many who have heard Skylarks dominate the farmland skies this seems incredible, as memory insists that we must have walked through fields for hours on end with the songs of Skylarks never letting up for a moment. What no doubt happens is that, where these birds are common, we hear the songs of many different Skylarks overlapping. Together they create an incessant background of sound that appears to come from a single bird.

In recent years, this torrent of melody has begun to falter somewhat, with the solemn news that the Skylark is in severe decline in Britain. The hard facts make alarming reading: from 1967 to 1999, for example, the population of Skylarks on surveyed farmland fell by a whopping 57%. Millions of pairs have become hundreds of thousands, and one of our best-loved birds is apparently disappearing fast.

The reasons, as in all these cases of struggling farmland birds, are complex, interrelated ones. The Skylark's problems mirror those of many other species of arable land, and are evident in both its breeding rate and winter survival. As far as the latter is concerned, the wholesale switch to sowing cereal grains in autumn, instead of spring, has resulted in Skylarks losing out on autumn and winter stubble, a major food resource. The overall reduction in spillage from barns and farm machinery during harvest has also played its part.

The breeding season presents a special problem to Skylarks. They nest on the ground, already a perilous place because of its vulnerability to predators, so any additional factors compromising their success here are bound to spell trouble. The growing of winter wheat has one particularly unfortunate by-product: the sward grows so tall and thick by spring that the larks can no longer hide their nests amidst the mini-forest, as would be ideal, but are forced to use the ruts and sill between rows, where they are much easier for predators to find. The impenetrable crop also decreases the density of Skylark territories, since it affords them fewer places to nest. Winter-planted crops, therefore, are probably a major cause in the Skylark's decline.

The cause, though, is far from lost. Skylarks are so popular, and their decline has spawned such an outcry, that the conservation agencies have dutifully plunged themselves into study pro-grammes to get to the heart of the bird's ecology. As a result, the Skylark's requirements are now well understood: it needs a diversity of adjacent crops in the breeding season, a little like the rotation farming of old, so that it can raise enough broods in different fields to maintain the population. In recent years, Skylark fortunes have also been aided by the introduction of set-aside, which introduces this sort of diversity. So, although there has not yet been an appreciable reverse of the decline, the fate of the Skylark seems much rosier than that of many of its colleagues in this beleaguered habitat.

This is certainly just as well. The Skylark may be an overrated songster, but its symbolic value for the countryside touches the same dizzy heights that it reaches in its aerial perambulations. Losing it would be unthinkable.

Pheasants and their harems

HOWEVER AMBIVALENT you might feel about Pheasants, perhaps because of the way that they were introduced to Britain in Norman times and even now don't quite seem to fit into our subtly-hued countryside, there's no doubt that the males of these birds make a stunning sight. With their over-ripe coloration and luxuriant, trailing tails, they are both unmistakable and unmissable. It comes as no surprise that they are related to that equally incongruous dandy, the Peacock. And there can be little doubt that, the moment a frumpish female Pheasant passes its eye over that fabulous feathered bling, it must start to tremble inside at the visual feast before it.

Wrong. Female Pheasants, it appears, aren't the slightest bit interested in the male's plumage. They are after more basic stuff. What really sets their pulses racing, it seems, are the male's dangly bits – the red wattles on his face. Apparently, these wattles inflate when a male is excited, and their width bears a direct correlation to the physical condition and testosterone levels of the bird con-cerned. The wattles also have black points on them, which become more conspicuous as they inflate, and the overall change in the male's head ornaments is what sets the female's desire aflame. All that fine feathering is great, but it serves only to make the male gender irresistible as a whole, rather than separating the men from the boys.

Well, at least the female has some choice at this point in the proceedings, which is more than can be said for the rest of her breeding season. Once she has picked a male – which is probably quite fun – it's all toil and trouble from then on. First, she lays one of the biggest clutches of any British bird: anything from eight to fifteen eggs. Then, she sits on them so tightly that it takes a remarkably vigilant predator to spot her. Finally, from the moment her chicks hatch, she tends all of them for several weeks and is completely responsible for their safety. It's hard work, the life of the single parent.

The plumage coloration of male and female Pheasant could hardly be more different.

But as we know, guys, there's a good reason for delegating all the parental duties to the female. Remember, Pheasants are ground dwellers that make excellent eating: just ask a fox, a dog or any member of the landed gentry. Everything carnivorous is after them. You simply cannot place that gaudy plumage next to a plump female with eggs or chicks; it would draw far too much atten-tion. Males that consort with their females are inviting trouble.

In Pheasant society, you see, the relationship between male and female is all about genetics, and nothing about partnership, and in a way this simplifies everything. The female is freed from expecting a contribution towards parental care from the male. This means that she can choose a mate based solely upon what he has to offer as a stud, as opposed to any fatherly qualities he might exhibit. So, although all that solo incubation and childcare may be a bit of a pain, at least the females know they will be producing high-quality offspring. Those wattles tell them so.

Another result of this simple relationship is that several females can share the charms of the same individual male without any conflict of interest. Since all the girls are getting from the male is sperm, and there is a surplus of this on offer, they do not find themselves fighting over his attention or assistance, or anything else that females of other species might require. There is no need for them, therefore, to get het up about infidelity, when fidelity has no currency. So it raises no eyebrows when male Pheasants gather more females and assemble a small harem. This is how Pheasants organise things, and a harem is the male's reward – so to speak – for being the fine specimen that he is.

Thus, many of the male Pheasants that you see in spring tend to be accompanied by two or more females. Some of the very finest acquire more than that – eighteen has been recorded – and many, conversely, acquire none at all. It is all brutally meritocratic: the best males get the most mates, and pass on their genes; the worst males get none, and merely pass the time.

Inevitably, though, it is seldom as simple as that. After all, how do you think a male builds up his harem in the first place? He is not like a red deer stag, running around trying to keep his flighty females on side; that would be far too dangerous. Instead, male Pheasants in early spring patrol along woodland edges, laying claim to a territory with a loud crowing call accompanied by a vigorous flapping. This call delineates a male's patch and, at the same time, invites females along for a road test, so to speak. If the females like what they see, they cuddle up, move in and spend enough time with the male to become inseminated and produce their large clutches. But the process is quite informal: the females are free to come and

Male Pheasants are unsubtle about their rivalry.

go as they like, and they change territories at will. Eventually, though, each settles down and stays within the borders of one male.

The males, not surprisingly, defend their territories vigorously, but they are not the most mobile of birds – they get around mostly on foot – and cannot be everywhere all of the time. This, unfortunately, allows them to be plagued by disenfranchised males, who lurk on the edges of their territory and are forever looking to molest the incumbent females. These "satellite" males, with chips on their shoulder, can be exceedingly disruptive to a breeding attempt, and have been known to kill eggs and young.

Sometimes, of course, territory owner and satellite meet, and these encounters are neither friendly nor pretty. Pheasants are fitted with sharp spurs on their feet, and, when fights break out, each birds turns these weapons on its opponent. If you've ever been attacked by a cockerel, you'll know only too well the sort of damage that spurs can inflict.

The satellite almost always loses, and beats a retreat. And as it does so, it might well reflect that wattles aren't the only measure of a male Pheasant's prowess: spurs are, too. The longest-spurred birds are the most successful and highest in rank. It may not seem fair, but at least it keeps things simple.

HILLS AND MOUNTAINS

Birds with altitude

BRITAIN'S MOUNTAINS are not very impressive in statistical terms. Indeed, if you were to confess to a Swiss or an Italian that our highest peak is only 1344m, you might receive a contemptuous snort. 'But we have supermarkets and libraries at that altitude,' they might say, incredulously. And they'd be right. But what our mountains lack in height, they make up for in their sheer terrifying climate.

SPEAK TO any ornithologist from across the Channel and you can put them in their place. 'Your mountains might be higher than ours,' you can argue, 'but we have breeding Snow Buntings'. That should restore some pride. The Snow Bunting breeds farther north than any other small bird, and in some of the most inhospitable places on earth. Many come down from high latitudes to spend the winter on our mountaintops, which have been evacuated by almost every other bird because of the severity of the weather. And if some stay all year and breed, then you can take this as a ringing endorsement that we have mountains to be reckoned with. Snow Buntings like it tough.

If we can define a landscape by the kind of birds that live there, then quite a lot of Britain – especially Scotland – qualifies as "uplands". Vast tracts of land are covered by open heather moorlands, blanket bogs and high grassland, and are dotted with rugged hills, often with cliffs and rocky slopes. Never mind the actual altitude, these are places vacated by "normal" birds in winter; the Grey Wagtails, Meadow Pipits and Song Thrushes disappear downhill in large numbers, leaving only the hardier species to cope with the wind, wet and cold. Thus, if most of

Left: Ptarmigans only occur in the harshest environments.

Previous spread: A flurry of Snow Buntings in the High Tops.

the birds travel downhill in autumn, then these places must surely count as uplands – at least ornithologically speaking.

Nevertheless, there is an important point to make here. Many of these patches of wild, open country would eventually be overgrown by woodland if the grazing sheep and deer were removed. And if that happened, then some of the retreating birds would remain behind in winter. For this reason we must label such places as "sub-montane". Only above this height, from 700m upwards, does the climate naturally exclude trees and restrict other plant growth to little more than turf height, thus making the habitat indisputably "montane". And this zone holds a selection of birds found nowhere else in Britain, whose special adaptations show them to be the true representatives of their lofty habitat.

Snowshoes

The best known of Britain's montane birds is a member of the grouse family called the Ptarmigan. It is famous for adopting a different plumage for each season of the year: in summer it is a delicate mottled golden colour to blend in with the lichens, mosses and cushion-plants; in autumn it assumes a greyer, more tired colour to match the fading season; in winter it turns a shocking white, becoming almost invisible against the snow-drifts; and in spring the golden-brown and white intermix, as if the white plumage was itself melting away to reveal the new growth underneath. And when it comes to coping with the climate, the Ptarmigan is no less impressively prepared. Like many cold climate birds, it has more layers of feathers than other birds, helping to keep it permanently warm. Even exposed extremities such as legs, feet and nostrils are covered with feathers. Nothing is left to chance. With this battery of defences, the Ptarmigan is capable of surviving at a latitude of 83°, far north of the Arctic Circle.

Feathered feet also have another advantage. The feathers increase the surface area of the toes, which helps to distribute the Ptarmigan's weight and make it less liable to sink in the soft snow. In winter, moreover, the toes grow long claws to exaggerate this effect and ensure that the Ptarmigan essentially walks around in snowshoes. This bird is an inveterate seeker of snow: in spring, where the area covered by snow begins to shrink, it seeks out a snowfield in which to bed down and roost. In short, it is one hardy grouse.

The Snow Bunting, sharing the tops with the Ptarmigan, also seeks snowfields, but for different reasons. In spring in particular, newly emerged

insects are often blown by the wind onto the surface of the snow. As soon as they touch the freezing crystals they are rendered almost immobile, their cold-blooded little bodies requiring heat to get them going again. This puts them at the mercy the Snow Buntings, who tuck in without even having to chase around.

The Snow Bunting is a tough little bird, never straying far from snowfields.

Snow Buntings have unusually thick plumage, like the Ptarmigan, but they do not have feathered feet. Instead, they employ a peculiar habit of crouching while feeding on ground, flexing their legs and thus ensuring that the ample belly feathers provide the naked skin with some protection.

There is only one other species in Britain that is truly montane, and that therefore will simply not breed downhill of about 800m. This is the Dotterel, which – by contrast to the Snow Bunting and Ptarmigan – is a seasonal visitor to the heights, arriving in May and leaving in August. Although it is healthily feathered, it is not specially adapted to the cold. What lures the Dotterel up here is the delicate mossy and lichen-covered ground of the montane zone. Though technically a wader, with the long legs and long, pointed wings of all its kind, this bird never actually gets its feet wet. Instead it tiptoes over the rocks and cushion plants, searching for surface-feeding invertebrates.

Trouble on the tops

The Dotterel, Snow Bunting and Ptarmigan are the only species in Britain confined to the montane zone, but they are not the only birds you might see up there. Other species with wider habitat portfolios also occur, including the Raven, Golden Eagle and Golden Plover. You might also see small birds such as Meadow Pipits and Wheatears, which can only survive here in the summer, starting their breeding season much later than they do at lower altitudes.

Ravens are mighty, buzzard-sized members of the Crow family, which often come up to the tops from the sheep country lower down. Montane conditions are no problem to them: they occur in a wider range of climatic conditions than just about any other species in the world, from the frozen north to the hottest deserts, and in Britain they span the complete altitudinal spread, from sea level to mountain top. Their success is down to versatility and guile, and the ability to exploit almost any feeding opportunity. On our mountains they tend mainly to scavenge from dead animals, but they can also be predatory, dispatching birds and mammals with their fearsome bill. Pairs sometimes co-operate when hunting, one member of the couple distracting the victim while the other goes in for the kill.

The astonishingly adaptable Raven occurs even up to the highest peaks.

A similar form of co-operation is often seen in the most impressive predator of the mountains, the Golden Eagle. Few animals stand much of a chance against one of these powerful birds hunting alone, let alone against a pair operating in tandem. Their technique is a very simple one: one bird flies low over the ground, using the contours of the hills to shield a surprise approach and causing its well-hidden prey to flush in sheer panic – straight into the talons of its partner. The two birds then share the meal.

Golden Eagles can fly in almost any conditions, and up here they need all their aerial skills because of the violence and changeability of the weather. These birds have more than two metres of wingspan to play with, and this gives them supreme mobility in the air, even in the most tempestuous of winds; they have been known to weather a 160kph gale, seemingly unruffled. Although the slow, low approach is the most favoured method of hunting, Golden Eagles have

plenty of other tricks in their repertoire. They can, for example, simply plunge down hundreds of metres on to an unsuspecting victim, wings folded back and lethal talons reaching forward. At other times they can snatch birds as small as Meadow Pipits from the sky. And, if circumstances demand it, they can even stalk their prey on foot.

In the montane zone two animals constitute the favoured prey of the Golden Eagle: the Mountain Hare and the Ptarmigan. The latter, indeed, can be the most abundant bird species hereabouts, and being quite plump and highly nutritious, it makes an excellent meal for a large predator. The eagle is famous for its keen eyesight – allegedly able to spot a Mountain Hare from a distance of at least 1000m – so the Ptarmigan's famed cryptic plumage is essential for survival under the spotlight of such ruthless surveillance.

As the top predator, the Golden Eagle can choose its prey, but is particularly partial to Mountain Hares.

The sub-montane zone

Below the 700m cut-off point, the sub-montane zone is a highly varied landscape. It includes large tracts of moorland, where Red Grouse hold sway, together with high sheep country, steep valleys and acid grassland. Birds breeding in this zone include such disparate species as Whinchats – a small, Robin-like species with a predilection for bracken-covered hillsides – and Lesser Black-backed Gulls, which nest on a few upland moors up to 20km from the sea. Other birds more familiar from lower altitudes, such as Meadow Pipits, Skylarks and Wrens, may also be abundant here, with Wheatears and Pied Wagtails being a little more localised in appearance.

There are some sub-montane species, however, which are fussy about the altitude at which they breed. One example is the Ring Ouzel. This handsome species resembles its close relative, the Blackbird, but with a white napkin tucked under

All tucked up – a Ring Ouzels' nest is placed in a sheltered spot.

its chin. It is almost always found above 250m, making it a true upland speciality and, further underlying these credentials, also occurs at high altitudes in the mountains of Central Europe. Ring Ouzels act like Blackbirds: they feed on the grass sward looking for worms and they pluck berries in the autumn. But they do it amidst the driving rain and zipping winds of areas inhospitable to their less hardy cousins.

Ring Ouzels, in common with a good many upland birds, are somewhat particular about where they place their nests. Getting a nest-site right is important to most birds, of course, but up here, because of the force of the weather, it is absolutely essential. For this reason Ring Ouzels almost always hold territories containing rocky outcrops, where they can hide their bulky nest away in a crevice, well protected. Some resourceful individuals have even been recorded raising

Bare ground is no obstacle to the hardy Twite.

their young in nests built inside mine shafts. The nest structure itself is designed for maximum protection, with a relatively wide girth and unusually thick walls.

Quite a few other upland birds also cater for the weather in their nest-building efforts. Wheatears, for example, sensibly select nest-holes whose entrance points away from the prevailing wind. And Ravens, which build very complex nests consisting of several different layers, make their cup especially deep when nesting in exposed places. Several other species nest close to rocks and irregularities to gain some shelter from the elements at ground level.

Up here, even a member of the largely arboreal finch family makes its nest on the ground. Whilst the more familiar members of this family, such as Chaffinch and Greenfinch, invariably build their intricate cups in trees and bushes, the Twite, a close relative of the Linnet, cannot rely on there being enough trees present at this altitude. Instead, this small, scarce bird seeks out rocky ledges, or patches of dense, low herbage, where the wind is deflected overhead.

The Twite has a very odd distribution – not just in our country, but in global terms, too. In Britain it is found in rugged regions of North and West Scotland, and also in a small separate outpost of 200–400 pairs in the Pennines, with nothing in between. Mirroring this disjunct distribution, Twites are also found in only two very different places worldwide: in the mountains and maritime zones of Britain and Scandinavia, and on the high plateaux and cold steppes of central Asia. Presumably, these patterns result from the gradual reduction in what was previously a much broader distribution during the last ice age, now reduced to relict populations.

Even so, the existence of the Twite simply reinforces the point we ornithologists can make to our Continental counterparts about Snow Buntings. With such special birds as Twites about, even our sub-montane zone demands respect.

Cain and Abel

UP IN the commanding and capacious eyries of Golden Eagles, unspeakable things occur. In a fierce habitat where life is always a battle and there are many losers, these lofty platforms, overlooking views fit for a king, routinely witness the cruellest and seemingly most senseless of deaths. The "Cain and Abel conflict" is a widely described aspect of eagle behaviour, but it is one that has continually left scientists baffled. Even highly trained and supposedly dispassionate professionals find themselves saddened at the pointlessness of it all.

The Golden Eagle is a very large bird that routinely lays two eggs. As is typical among most birds of prey, the female begins incubation as soon as the first egg is laid, kick-starting the development of the youngster inside. If all goes well, a second egg comes along anything between three or four days later and it, too, is immediately warmed by the brood patch of the adult, setting its own development in train.

By beginning incubation as soon as the first egg is laid, the female generally gives its first-born an advantage in life. Each egg needs roughly the same length of time to bring its inhabitant to readiness for hatching, so the second egg invariably hatches three or four days later than the first. This means that the first chick will have had several meals by the time its sibling hatches, and will already be touching a weight of 250g – more than twice that of the newborn chick. The scene is set for an uneven contest.

It is not unusual for birds to practise what is known technically as asynchronous hatching, in which the ages of chicks in a single brood differ. Many species do it; it offers them an insurance strategy. When an adult feeds its chicks, it will instinctively offer food to the individual that begs in the most vigorous fashion, notwithstanding the fact that this may cause aggression and bullying among the brood. Only when the bully is satiated will the adult serve its less vigorous chicks, while their nemesis dozes. The frequency of offerings to the weaker, younger birds is of course directly related to how quickly the eldest chick gets its fill; and that, concomitantly, depends on how much food is available. By allowing chicks of varying ages to compete within the brood, an adult bird can ensure that at least one chick survives, even in times of food shortage, since it will always get first pick. If that same adult were

democratic in its offerings at times of shortage, all the chicks would have an equal amount of not enough. Thus all would perish and nesting would be a failure. However, in times of plenty, all the chicks might survive, despite the imbalances in their age and strength.

The aim of having differently-aged chicks in a brood, therefore, is to ensure that life's inequality plays out, one way or the other. The system is also known, rather unfeelingly, as brood reduction. We might not like the idea, but it certainly makes sense.

What happens in a Golden Eagle nest, however, is something different. When the second egg in a brood hatches, the older sibling doesn't just overwhelm it by grabbing all the food, it does something much more decisive: it kills it. Yes, believe it or not, in about of 80% of Golden Eagle nests Cain, the first-born, kills Abel, the second born. This siblicide usually, but not always occurs within a few hours of the second egg hatching. There is little or no time for good old fashioned competition.

So all we know about brood reduction falls here. Why on earth should murder routinely take place in the nest? Many theories have been advanced, including various suggestions about food supply. But the killings are not confined to seasons when food is short. Indeed, among some of the Golden Eagle's close relatives, such as the Lesser Spotted Eagle of Europe and Asia, the first born invariably kills its rival, without any heed to circumstance at all.

Let's look at some more theories. Could the second bird be an extra meal for its sibling, offering some much needed early protein? Hardly: the second bird is often not eaten. Could the second egg be insurance against the first one not hatching? This is the most widely quoted theory. But if that was so, why don't the parents wait until the second egg hatches before starting incubation? Or why don't they wait longer than three or four days between eggs, to see how the first bird gets on in its early life?

The more you look at it, the more the mystery deepens. Some have suggested that the siblicide may work in favour of female birds, occurring

The parent Golden Eagle is attentive at the nest, but does nothing to prevent the killing.

when a female hatches first, and thus skewing the sex ratio in favour of the female birds, whose survival rates are lower. But no measurements of sex ratio in broods support this, which throws it out of court for the moment.

So what on earth causes this apparently point-less bloodshed? One day, we will know. In the meantime we can muse on an intriguing thought: Golden Eagles occur in the Holy Lands, so perhaps, on the very day that Cain actually slew Abel, the exact same thing was happening on a nearby Biblical cliff-top.

They stoop to conquer

THE MOST successful predators are not always the biggest. The bird of prey, indeed, that has truly taken over the world is neither as large as an Eagle nor as formidable as a Goshawk. Remarkably, it looks little larger than a Kestrel.

You can tell this bird is something awesome by the reaction of other birds to it. A group of waders or ducks feeding in the open will often not react much to a Kestrel, and may only pay passing attention to a Buzzard. But if a Peregrine is overhead, everybody panics. Birds rush hither and thither, at high speed, going nowhere much at all. They call loudly to one another as they dash about, yet their haste and energy is often wasted. The Peregrine watches the palaver from high above, and often simply moves on to cause panic somewhere else. This supreme predator always has plenty of options.

The terror engendered by the Peregrine is understandable: few other birds can feel safe when it takes to the skies. These remarkable hunters have been known to catch 120 different species in Britain alone, which is half of all our breeding species – and these are just the ones that we've been able to record. The victims range in size from the tiny Goldcrest to the huge Heron, so every bird – bar perhaps a Golden Eagle – must always be on its guard.

The other aspect of the Peregrine that provokes such fear is the way in which it kills. Birds know that this hunter can strike from almost anywhere, without warning. Just because the Peregrine is a thousand metres above ground or several kilometres away, that doesn't make you safe. No, the Peregrine is dangerous at any distance, because it is quite simply the fastest moving bird – indeed possibly the fastest moving creature of any kind – in the world.

When a Peregrine has spotted some likely prey, which it might do while perched on a crag or circling at high altitude, its strategy is generally to strike from above. So it manoeuvres itself to a point high above what it hopes is its unsuspecting quarry and then, once in position, simply plunges down towards its prey, with wings almost folded. Allowing gravity to work, the bird soon accelerates to quite astonishing speeds. If the dive – or "stoop" as it is usually known – is from about 1000m up, then in theory a peregrine weighing 1kg could accelerate to more than 300kph. So far no speed of more than 180kph has ever been confirmed. Nevertheless, that is pretty fast.

But the bald statistics do not capture the full drama of the Peregrine's stoop, which is one of the great sights of birdwatching. You see the hunter circle in the sky, note its sudden concentration, and then watch as, almost casually, it begins to close its wings and drop. With a few full flaps to power its dive, the Peregrine is soon at the mercy of its own gravity. You simply cannot believe that a bird can move so fast.

One might expect that a Peregrine would dive vertically, but this isn't always the case. On longer drops, especially, it usually maintains an angle of 30–45° to the vertical. The reason for this is that a Peregrine's overlapping, binocular vision – the zone of vision most effective for judging distance – works best at an angle of 40° to its target. And so, rather than tilting its head, which would increase drag, the Peregrine dives at a slant.

The dive not only gets the Peregrine to its target very quickly, but also creates enormous momentum. This means that Peregrines don't usually need to dispatch their prey with a bite to the back of the head, as most falcons do, but simply kill it on impact. Usually all you see is a fast-moving Peregrine and then a puff of feathers as the talons – balled into fists – strike the bird. The victim's neck is often broken, and occasionally the poor creature is decapitated. Compared with the messy exploits of many a bird

Hidden terror – a Peregrine sits and scans.

of prey, this kind of kill is swift and decisive and, in a way, almost merciful.

No Peregrine would admit to a mercy killing, though. These are predators at the very top of the food chain; they kill birds for a living, every day, often several times a day. In the mountains they specialise on pigeons, often commuting to the lowlands to find them, but many also feed closer at hand on Ptarmigans and other mountain dwellers. As mentioned earlier, Peregrines can kill almost everything.

With its devastating and simple killing technique, the Peregrine has become the king of bird predators in every way. Not only does it terrorise our birds throughout Britain, but also on every major continent of the world. Peregrines kill birds in North and South America, and in Asia, Australia and Africa. No other diurnal bird of prey – perhaps no other land bird at all – has as wide a natural distribution.

And incredibly, among the 10,000 species of birds in the world, the Peregrine is estimated to have tasted more than 1000. That's ten percent of all the birds in the world. So, if all those are the Peregrine's subjects, that's evidence enough of who is king.

The hooded executioner strikes a pigeon.

Girls on top

SHORT BREEDING seasons make birds do odd things. Up in the Arctic, for example, some birds turn up on their territories so early that the tundra has not yet thawed and there is no food available for them to eat. Others treat the brief summer as if it were an orgy, the males trying to copulate with every female in sight. Still others lay as many eggs as possible as quickly as possible, and allow some to be incubated by birds that are almost strangers. It's all caused by a shortage of time; the need to squeeze the demanding schedule of reproduction into a brief window of opportunity.

On mountains, the same rule applies. The season is shorter than in the foothills and lowlands, and there is a similar precipitous rush to get breeding moving as fast as possible. So, not surprisingly, some montane birds get up to a few tricks of their own.

But few mountain birds are quite so odd in their breeding habits as a small plover-like bird called the Dotterel. It's a bit smaller than a Lapwing, but it has a similar big head, large eye, short bill and long, slightly spindly legs. Like the Lapwing it feeds by running in stop-start fashion over short turf, watching still for the movement of insects on the surface, and then dashing off to grab what it has seen. The only difference is that the Dotterel swaps the Lapwing's agricultural fields for barren, rocky, short-turfed mountain plateaux, and is rarely found below 800 metres.

Another important difference is that, while the Lapwing follows the avian norm of the male being larger and more colourful than the female, in the Dotterel things are the other way round. The female has the more splendid and colourful plumage. And this quirk is not just incidental. The female wears the badge in accordance with her status. In the Dotterel's world, the women are the strong ones, while the males have assumed the gentler, nurturing role.

This role reversal begins early in the breeding cycle, when it is the females, rather than the males, who take the initiative in courtship. Almost as soon as they arrive on the hilltops, Dotterels form mixed sex flocks. Somewhat unsubtly, the females cast their eyes over the males in the flock. If they are taken by a particular individual, they will run after him and attempt to isolate him from the others, in full view of everyone. If this doesn't work, a female will make her own little run away from the flock

A female Dotterel (third from left) gets flirtatious. A group of Dotterels is known as a "trip".

and squat down, pretending to be on eggs, attempting to lure her desired away. If this works, great. But it must be pretty embarrassing if the male just stands his ground and refuses to move.

Inevitably, perhaps, there is much bickering in these flocks over who pairs off with whom; after all, in any population of animals some will be better looking than others. In Dotterels both sexes fight amongst themselves, female against female, male against male, until, eventually, after much frustration, pairs officially form. Some localities often have an uneven sex ratio, which leaves some birds frustrated – at least for the moment.

The pair bond is a fragile and short-lived thing. Male Dotterels, constantly afraid that their

paternity will be compromised, copulate with their mate with unseemly frequency, trying to flood out the sperm of any male that might have inseminated the female in secret. And they have good cause to be cautious. Not only are female Dotterels a bit skittish, but the male is about to make an immense investment of time and energy as a father, and he does not wish to waste his efforts on somebody else's offspring.

It is once the eggs are laid, however, that the male enters into the ultimate role reversal: from now on, he will be the lone caring parent. The female, for her part, may remain in touch if the clutch is lost, but she will take no further interest in the eggs she has just laid. On the contrary, in

order to maximise her breeding potential for the season, she may well find another male with whom to form another short association and lay a second clutch. In this case, males that were frustrated earlier may well find their breeding season turning the corner.

Thus, for almost a month, the male incubates the eggs alone, taking on the personal effort and peril usually borne by a female bird. It is he that calls to the chicks when they are still in the egg, waiting for the fruits of his encouragement to hatch out. It is he who remains in place while rain, mist and snow – frequent bedfellows to a brooding Dotterel – must be endured. It is he who leads the chicks away from the nest site after they hatch, and tends them as they grow, and calls to them to sit still when danger threatens. And it is he who will, if necessary, divert predators from the chicks by crouching down and running away, pretending to be a small mammal. He performs all these tasks alone, with no help from the female at all. And indeed, if she does make an appearance, he sometimes aggressively shoos her away.

As for most females, they leave their eggs in the care of males and, in the best traditions of parents without responsibilities, wander off to look after themselves. They depart the breeding sites early, and find a safe place to feed and moult. In human terms this behaviour is equivalent to treating themselves to a spot of pampering at a health farm. It makes for a relaxing end to a short and undemanding breeding season.

So, emancipated female dotterels live by the maxim 'girls on top'. And they wouldn't want it any other way.

This male Dotterel has a hard breeding season ahead.

STILL WATER

Water, water, everywhere

AWAY FROM our gardens and urban areas, still water is probably the habitat we know best. Most of us first learnt about birds on lakes when, as children, our parents took us to feed the ducks; and even the least attentive of us must have noticed that besides ducks, there are also such things in the world as swans and gulls. Yet in our familiarity, we should not overlook the important point that not all ponds and lakes in Britain are the same. The moorland lakes of Northern Scotland have little in common with the urban ponds of the English lowlands, and neither have their birds.

THE OPEN freshwater habitats of Britain are astonishingly varied in their appearance, chemistry, origin and use. There are big lakes and tiny ponds; natural glacial lakes and lakes carved out by human hand; deep lakes and shallow lakes; acidic lakes and alkaline lakes. Most importantly, there are lakes full of birds and lakes that are almost bird-free. It seems obvious to say so, but every pool, pond and lake in Britain is slightly different from every other, and this can make open freshwater a difficult habitat to interpret. But if we look at each characteristic of a water body in turn, we find patterns that explain which birds are there and why. Once we understand these patterns, we realise that it is actually possible to read a lake simply by its birds.

We must start by looking at a lake's biological productivity, since this is what truly sorts out the bird-filled habitats from those with a lot of vacant water. The concept may sound complicated, but it boils down to how many plants can grow in the water. If there are lots of plants, both in the water and along the edge, then there are usually lots of birds, too.

The acid test

It is essentially chemistry that determines whether water offers a welcoming habitat for plants. The lake's bedrock and soil influences the amount of nutrients in its waters, and where these are limited, so is the plant life. The lakes amid the highly acidic moorlands of Northern Scotland, for example, are pretty useless for birds. In these inhospitable waters, only a limited suite of plants can grow. These play host to a restricted number of plant-eaters, such as insects or molluscs and, in turn, there are few fish or other predators. Thus one of the few breeding species on these impoverished waters, the fish-eating Red-throated Diver, habitually commutes from the safety of its private loch to the sea to find enough food for its young.

Although the highly acidic lochans in the far north of Scotland are extreme examples, most of the more unproductive – or, to be scientific, oligotrophic – lakes in Britain are found in Northern England or Scotland. While their water chemistry is the deciding factor in the birds they attract, the nature of the surrounding countryside is also important. Many oligotrophic lakes are found at altitude, often on bleak hills battered by

Previous spread: A rich winter wetland, with Mallards, Teal, Mute Swans and Tufted Ducks.

Above: Stranger on the water – many birdwatchers have never seen a Red-throated Diver in the wild.

Lake birds are easy to see and enjoy.

wind and rain. Here heavy waves make it difficult for plants to gain a foothold along their banks. The waters, therefore, have bare, rocky shores almost devoid of plant life or shelter. These lakes are often large, too, which means that winds can tear over their surface and give any visiting birds a rough ride.

Nonetheless, birds do occur on oligotrophic lakes, and these are attracted by yet another defining characteristic of a lake: the clarity of the water. The lack of nutrient-rich soil, together with the fact that such lakes are usually deep, combines to create a large, uncluttered, clear water environment. These conditions are ideal for fish-chasing species such as the Goosanders, the Red-breasted Merganser, Divers – including the rare Black-throated Diver – and the Slavonian Grebe. All these birds submerge below the surface and have feet set well back on their bodies, enabling them to kick hard and build up a good speed underwater. The small Slavonian Grebe, for example, can swim at more than a kilometre an hour. Though relatively few fish may live in Oligotrophic lakes, these birds are well adapted for catching the ones that do.

Richer waters

Fortunately for resident bird-watchers, the majority of lakes in the southern half of Britain are not oligotrophic, but "eutrophic" – which means productive. Their geology makes them highly fertile and full of nutrients, supporting a wide variety and quantity of aquatic plants, and thus they tend to be well stocked with birds. Where the surrounding countryside offers shelter, a rich fringe of vegetation, from emergent reeds to well-established alder or willow trees, can also

form, and this adds to their appeal and diversity.

Within the eutrophic category, however, there are still considerable differences between water bodies. Some are rather obvious: larger lakes, for example, have room for higher numbers of birds. They can potentially support more species than smaller ones can, too, since the greater area enables the shyer species to swim well away from disturbance. Similarly, a varied shoreline or the presence of islands also boosts the diversity: breeding ducks, for example, usually nest on islands because these provide security from predators and undisturbed vegetation in which to hide their nests. A long, convoluted shoreline also provides coves and shallows where other birds can hide away.

The way that people use lakes can also define their potential. Lowland lakes may be used for power boating (usually a disaster for birds) or for angling, or any number of other pursuits. The simple presence of close humanity on a lake-side footpath is too much for some species, such as Goosanders. Conversely, kind folk provide food for the wildfowl on some ponds and lakes, and this may have some benefit, if not in attracting new birds, then at least in allowing them to become used to people. Further down the line, those children excited by an encounter with ducks or swans may become birdwatchers – and perhaps even conservationists.

Duck detectives

Away from the broad categories, individual lakes have subtle characteristics that suit certain species and not others. And it is here that we can become detectives, discovering the properties of a lake simply by watching and counting the birds that

reside there. Any birdwatcher can do this with just a small amount of knowledge.

To start with, a rough rule of thumb gives us a good idea of a lake's depth. If we see Tufted Ducks and Pochards on a lake, we can confidently proclaim to astonished friends that this lake must be at least two metres deep. Both these species are diving ducks; they tend to avoid shallow water, where they become somewhat restricted. This is not rocket science, but it can be enough to make us hold our children's hands a little tighter as we walk them round the edge. If we see fish-pursuing Great Crested Grebes, we can also deduce that the lake has deeper areas unclogged with vegetation. And if the lake is frequented by Goosanders in the winter, it is probably deeper still and we would not like to capsize a boat upon it. Beyond 15m, the lake will lose its Tufted Ducks, which are unwilling to dive this deep for food.

The presence of each of these species confirms, logically enough, that their favourite foodstuffs must also be there. Both Great Crested Grebes and Goosanders feed mainly upon fish. The grebe will take anything from a stickleback 3cm long to an eel 20cm long, while the Goosander usually catches fish of less than 11cm in length. The two commonest diving ducks have completely different diets: Pochards, as a rule, feed mainly on plant material gained from dives to the bottom; Tufted Ducks prefer animal food, especially molluscs. Thus Tufted Ducks can tolerate lakes without much aquatic vegetation, while Pochards prefer their water to be clogged with the stuff. And for those who really want to play the detective, scientists have recently discovered that male Pochards tend to feed in deeper water than females, so the distribution of the sexes around the lake could give you a further clue to its submarine topography.

Another common diving bird on lakes is the Coot. This coal-black, duck-like species lacks the fully webbed feet and flattened bill of ducks, and actually belongs in the Rail family. Like the Pochard, it feeds on vegetation from the bottom, usually descending just a couple of metres – though it will go down to about 6m at a stretch. In common with some other submerging birds, you can gauge the depth to which it is diving by the way it goes under. Coots usually dive with a forward leap, and the higher and more vertical the leap, the deeper the dive.

Surface feeders

The distinction between these diving birds and those that only work the surface is important. Surface feeders, as you might expect, tend to avoid deep water when feeding – although they might use it for roosting and loafing. So the presence of birds such as Gadwall and Shoveler on a lake tells you that large stretches of the water must be less than 2m deep, and often much less. These two ducks both depend on highly productive lakes, but the dietary differences between them mirror those between the Pochard and the Tufted Duck. The Gadwall is a confirmed vegetarian, only ever taking plant material and almost always gathering it while swimming in the shallows. Its preferred method of feeding is simply to immerse its head and neck from a swimming position and pluck shoots and leaves in situ. The Shoveler, on the other hand, feeds mostly on plankton and small animals. It is the archetypal "dabbler", using the tip of its bill to filter food from the surface, and prefers shallow water, where there is usually a richer suspension of food.

Our smallest duck, the Teal, avoids competition with other ducks by feeding in the shallowest water of all, often just a few centimetres deep at

A lake with Tufted Ducks will have water at least 2m deep but less than 15m.

the very edge of the lake. Indeed, it is commonly seen walking along the lakeshore, dipping its bill at the point at which the water laps on to the mud or stranded weed. It will also immerse its neck in these same shallows. In winter the Teal tends to search for seeds, sieving them from the water or mud. Their abundance often allows a Teal to feed for long periods in the same spot.

Perhaps surprisingly, quite a few ducks can find a meal without ever getting their feet wet. The Wigeon, a prime example, feeds almost entirely on grass. This food, of course, does not grow underwater, so if Wigeon are consistently present on a lake, you can be sure that there is some undisturbed grazing available nearby. A short bill and a strong jawbone help Wigeon to tug out grass from the earth. They often feed in tight groups, moving slowly forward across the sward, like a flock of brightly coloured, waddling sheep.

Long necks and loud mouths

Wigeons are not the only lake birds to feed on grass. Canada Geese and Mute Swans do, too, and the laziest of Wigeons will occasionally stand

next to these tall birds and field whatever edible fragments drop from their bills. The Canada Goose, of course, is not the most popular of lake inhabitants, although our habit of maintaining wide grassy stretches around ornamental lakes is the perfect encouragement for this handsome bird. It was introduced to Britain from the New World in the 17th Century and, for the first couple of centuries or so it was the ideal guest: smart, well behaved and confined to the grounds of a few stately homes. Over the last fifty years, however, its population has greatly increased and now, with the exotic veneer having long since worn thin, it has become fashionably unpopular. People mutter "pest" and "vermin" and vow to destroy it. It can certainly damage crops and grass, but other charges against it, such as the assertion that it is a health hazard and that it out-competes native wildfowl, are not backed by strong evidence and are little more than trumped-up claptrap. Of course, the Canada Goose is noisy, sometimes intimidating, and defecates with frequency and gusto, but it does little harm other than to some people's delicate sensibilities.

Canada Geese are one of a number of lake birds to have been introduced to Britain from overseas.

A Wigeon snatches a bite from a grazing swan.

A long tradition of collecting wildfowl for pleasure and prestige has ensured that many waters, especially those close to built-up areas, hold unfamiliar duck-billed faces from various parts of the world. These include Red-crested Pochards from Europe, Wood Ducks from North America, Egyptian Geese from Africa and Mandarin Ducks from Asia, all of which sometimes breed in the wild. The gorgeous Mandarin Duck has built up a population of at least 7,000 birds in Britain, and this now constitutes nearly 10% of the entire world population of this fairly scarce species.

The Mandarin Duck brings us back to considering the varying properties of lakes. You might have thought that a lake deep within a wood would be a good place for birds, but you'd be wrong. A lining of trees can make a small lake difficult to get at for some lake species, and it seems, too, that the claustrophobic shoreline makes the visitors nervous, worrying that it provides easy cover for lurking predators. But it is just this kind of place that suits the small, fast-flying, highly manoeuvrable Mandarin, and here, alone among "British" ducks, it thrives. On autumn nights, this character often ventures into the nearby woods to pick up acorns and other seeds.

In a sense, the Mute Swan is also a naturalised bird. Although native here in truly ancient times (remains at least two million years old have been found in East Anglia), it probably died out as a truly wild species by 1300 as a result of being over-hunted for food. A semi-domesticated population survived and, once the practice of eating swans died out, this formed the nucleus of the current thriving population. Mute Swans are among the most popular of lake birds and, despite being aggressive at times, their looks and charisma shield them from the abuse directed towards their Canadian neighbours. They are also quiet, if not actually mute. The wondrous loud sighing sound made by their wings means Mute Swans have no need to make loud contact calls in flight; all they do is hiss and sneeze.

Up-ending

The presence of Mute Swans is as instructive as that of any other lake birds about the nature of their habitat. They shun oligotrophic waters, since they feed mainly upon profuse plant growth, and they also lean towards lakes that have some grass or fields nearby, offering an alternative food source. The depth of the lake is also important: with their long necks, Mute Swans have a

The presence of Mallards on a lake gives nothing away.

competitive advantage over other waterfowl because they can reach down further and graze on submerged plant material out of range of all but Coots and Pochards. By dipping their necks from a swimming position they are already healthily competitive, but as often as not they perform a different contortion known as "up-ending". This is a floating equivalent of a hand-stand; the bird leans so far over into the water that it over-balances, with its head pointing down and its feet furiously paddling on the surface. From this position, a Mute Swan can reach down 90cm.

Other waterfowl, including most ducks, also up-end and thus increase the depth range over which they can forage. Only one species, though, really specialises in it: the Pintail, a bird tapered at both ends. With its long neck, this elegant duck can reach plant material, especially seeds, in ooze over 30cm below the surface, way out of reach of its main competitor, the diminutive Teal. With their fairly specialised requirements, Pintail are only found on selected waters.

There is one bird, however, whose presence tells us almost nothing about the characteristics of the water in which it swims. This is the most dominant of all characters on lakes and ponds: the ubiquitous Mallard. It is the most successful duck in the world, and this success is built on its ability to exploit almost any type of freshwater habitat – even some oligotrophic lakes. Mallards can feed in almost any depth. They can dabble, dip and up-end with the best of them, and their ten distinct methods of feeding include everything from grazing on land to, yes, taking bread from children. The Mallard is every duck for everywhere.

All you learn when you see a Mallard, therefore, is what is already obvious: somewhere, nearby, there is water.

Marriage guidance from swans

Mute Swans keep their inner fires burning by frequent display.

BRITAIN HAS an alarmingly high divorce rate – among humans, at least. It has been growing steadily since the 1940s, with all its concomitant misery and mess and now, at the beginning of the 21st century, about 40% of marriages end in this way. The trend has even begun to worry government agencies, producing solemn warnings about the social and economic consequences of family breakdown.

But if we had only looked out of our windows a few more times, or taken a walk down by the park, we might perhaps have absorbed some important lessons from the bird world. We should, you see, have been watching swans.

Swans are famously faithful to their mates. Several studies have shown that very few pairs, once hitched, ever split up. In the Mute Swan, the actual divorce rate is about 3% of established pairs; and in that of the closely related Bewick's Swan, a Russian bird that spends the winter here, it is only 1%. If we humans ever managed to attain that figure, one might assume that all our social problems would disappear and that our politicians could spend more time with their own families.

Clearly, swans are doing something right, and if we take a closer look at their breeding behaviour, who knows, perhaps we could pick up a few useful ideas for ourselves?*

The first trick that helps swans strengthen their relationships is not rushing into them. By contrast with most birds, swans mature quite slowly. They usually leave their parents at the start of their first winter, when they are perhaps four or five months old and still wearing brown or greyish plumage, and join a community of swans constituting a "non-breeding flock". These flocks are precisely as described: they are made up of non-breeding birds – mostly youngsters, but also adults without a territory and occasionally older birds, too. The cygnets will be members of this flock for at least two years. While enrolled they learn about all aspects of swan life, including both social and sexual behaviour, and thus they have plenty of time to become both individuals in their own right and participants in the wider swan community.

Only in their second year of membership do the cygnets indulge in any form of courtship, and it is only very innocent stuff – equivalent, perhaps, to the human stage of holding hands for the first time. Nevertheless, the youngsters' eyes are opened at this time to the attractions of the opposite sex. Indeed, it is highly likely that their desires will shift from the general to the specific, and they will begin to make eyes at certain individuals within their flock.

During the next season, many birds do pair off, and their subsequent behaviour is determined by the type of partner they take on. Three-year-old female swans are in high demand among males. They may quickly be snapped up by any widowers or divorcees in the local community, thus entering the adult world more quickly than the rest. Otherwise, should a pair of youngsters team up they will usually wait for yet another season before actually making a genuine attempt to breed. In effect, youngsters have an "engagement period", during which – in theory at least – they can swap their

*Note: the following advice is intended as a guide only; the author takes no responsibility for the actions of readers consequent to the suggestions herein.

51

partner's charms for those of another bird. Males often reach their fourth year before they are finally at the head of a family of chicks.

So Mute Swans appear to be cautious and unhurried when entering into a formal breeding unit. But that's not their only secret for a long-lasting relationship: another is to keep their internal fires burning.

Human beings tend to view courtship as what occurs before marriage, and spend little time on it thereafter. Mute Swans, in their wisdom, re-enter into intense courtship at the beginning of each breeding season, and their displays often continue throughout the spring and into early summer, only subsiding once breeding is over. They use a range of postures to keep reaffirming their commitment. The most famous is known as "head-turning", in which the two birds face each other with their breasts almost touching, and often their neck feathers ruffled and their wings slightly raised, too. As the partners meet in this way, it so happens that their arched necks make an attractive heart shape – inconsequential to them, but a pleasing sight to us.

Equally importantly, Mute Swans also maintain an active sex life. Copulation is frequent, and goes well beyond what is needed to fertilise the year's brood. So, as it is for us, the act of mating is recreational as well as procreational. It is an expression of commitment and a reaffirmation of desire. Year on year, it seems not to lose its frequency, and there is little doubt that it helps the birds to maintain their long-term relationship.

There is yet a third secret to the Mute Swan's faithfulness, and that is in the pair's committed and tender care of their youngsters. The parenting follows well-defined roles, which mirror the traditional ones of humans: the male is very much a protector, although he takes on some of the parenting chores, while the female is primarily involved in nurturing.

A good example of this division of labour occurs early in the season. The female takes on the incubation of the eggs herself, although

Mute Swans are devoted parents as well as loyal partners.

the male will sit on them when she is feeding. Meanwhile, the important task of keeping the territory safe from intruders and predators falls primarily to the male. The "cob" Mute Swan is a formidable sight when angry: it ruffles its neck and back feathers, lifts its wings, places its neck against its chest and charges towards a threat with two-footed swimming strokes. It will also hiss loudly. If this display doesn't work (it usually does) then the swan will also fight, grabbing the neck of its opponent in an attempt to drown it, or striking it with the "elbow" of its wings. Problem solved, the male returns to the nest and performs a triumph ceremony, lifting his chin and ruffling his feathers. The message is clear: the male celebrates his victory, and magnifies the mutual "us against the world" attitude of the pair.

Once the chicks have hatched, both parents assume rather similar tasks. Together they will take the cygnets for a ride on their backs (for protection rather than entertainment), pull up submerged waterweed to help them feed, and watch over them as they steadily grow. In other words, the parenting is very much teamwork right to the end.

And teamwork, of course, underpins all the Mute Swan's relationship skills. Before and during breeding, the birds remain together and never stop communicating. They work together and learn together, and their lives become inextricably intertwined. The outside world remains just that: outside.

That, then, is the Mute Swan's secret. How odd it should be that these big white birds embrace all the principles that we humans seek in love! Perhaps we should pay them a little more attention.

Say it with weed: water courtship in grebes

The Head-shaking Ceremony.

EVERY SPRING, a minor choreographic master-piece is enacted on the ponds and lakes of Britain. We pay the earth to watch great performances at Covent Garden, but this show is free; to see it, we need only pop down to our local park. And although, to scientists, this showpiece is one of the most famous bird spectacles in the world, it is scarcely known to the general public and often poorly appreciated even by bird enthusiasts.

The Great Crested Grebe is a common and good-looking waterbird that sustains itself by diving down from the surface to chase fish. In productive waters this is not a very arduous activity; the fish don't give themselves up, exactly, but it is not hard for a Great Crested Grebe to catch enough to get by. As a result, it spends a lot of time floating on the water; and, over the millennia, that relative idleness has allowed it plenty of free time in which to develop some highly sophisticated courtship manoeuvres. These ceremonies were originally described by Julian Huxley in 1914, and they became one of the very first bird displays to be investigated in any depth.

Huxley recognised four main types of routine, which he called "ceremonies", and within each one were individual manoeuvres or postures which he called "displays". The best known of the ceremonies, and the only one that is maintained throughout the breeding season, is known as "head-shaking". In the inimitably literal language of scientists, this refers to a display in which birds shake their heads. It is characteristic of pairs that may be greeting each other and therefore, in contrast to human gesture, a shake of the head probably means "yes". The birds face each other, making excited braying noises; with their head ornaments ruffled and neck fully extended, they waggle their heads from side to side, often at the same time lowering or raising their neck. During the more serious bouts of head-shaking, the performers intermittently break off and lean down to preen a feather on their back. Actually, this is only a gesture: the feather is not preened, but merely touched, and this display, known as "habit-preening", simply serves to embellish the main moves.

Head-shaking constitutes a separate ceremony on its own, but the physical manoeuvre itself is easy to perform and so often appears in other ceremonies, too. In an early-season display known as the "discovery ceremony", for example, it takes place right at the conclusion of the process.

The discovery ceremony is a complex display, but it is not hard to observe. Just wait by a lake in March and you should get at least one perform-ance out of your birds. It essentially involves the couple feigning an unexpected meeting, with one

The Discovery Ceremony.

bird creeping up behind the other and suddenly showing itself off, as if to say 'Here I am!' The routine begins with one of the pair approaching its partner underwater like a submarine, sticking its head up every so often, but also keeping its body so close to the surface that its wake is clearly visible. On observing this so-called "ripple approach", the other partner assumes an encouraging posture of its own, known as the "cat display", in which it spreads its facial fan-like plumes and holds its wings half open. Then, unexpectedly, the first bird disappears under the water, only to reappear, like a child in a swimming pool, behind the first bird, rearing up with its bill pointing skywards and effectively saying 'Boo!' Such is the impact of this "ghostly penguin display" that both birds come together to have a good head-shake and an approving growl.

The cat display also appears in a sort of reverse of this process, a sequence known as the "retreat ceremony". This set of manoeuvres is often triggered when an intruder has been evicted from the grebes' territory, and it is also characteristic of the early part of the season. It always begins with head-shaking, but this is then abruptly halted when one bird suddenly makes a low pattering flight over the water, either away from its partner or directly past, this being the eponymous "retreat". Having moved off a few metres, the bird assumes the cat display and then almost meekly turns back and faces its partner, perhaps red-faced at its own impetuousness. Both birds then come back together and head-shake. Sometimes, though, the second bird (usually the male) immediately takes its own turn in making the ritualised retreat.

But by far the most spectacular and exciting Great Crested Grebe ceremony is called the "weed ceremony". This is particularly dramatic because it builds up relatively slowly and then finishes with a dazzling climax. It is also quite sparingly performed, so that every time you see it you can consider yourself privileged.

Predictably, the weed ceremony begins with a sequence of intense head-shaking. This time, however, there is no abrupt interruption, as in the discovery ceremony or retreat ceremony. Instead the birds gently drift apart on the water, regularly habit-preening as though still face-to-face. Then, having apparently just noticed that they are no longer close together, they simultaneously dive. This is the point at which the observer should redouble concentration, for it is the trigger for what comes next.

If the birds remain underwater for some time, you can be pretty sure that both will surface with a clump of soft pondweed in the bill. Interestingly, they will always come up some metres apart as if,

Great Crested Grebes spend a lot of time Head-shaking, often calling loudly while doing it.

while out of sight, they were co-ordinating things with one another. At any rate, the two birds now swim quite determinedly towards one another, in a display known as the "weed-approach" (imaginative, these scientists). It's rather like the Cathy and Heathcliffe routine: both birds metaphorically running together open-armed into a loving embrace.

But the birds don't embrace. Instead, when the two partners reach each other, they both rear up out of the water and stand vertically upright, breast to breast, madly treading water to keep their balance and their pose – like two portly ballerinas trying not to fall off a floating platform. While doing so they "offer" their dangling pondweed to one another, swinging it in unison from side to side and gurgling excitedly as they do so.

And this exquisite spectacle, ladies and gentlemen, is the culmination of the Great Crested Grebe's display. It doesn't last for long, and soon both birds are back in their normal swimming posture, Head-shaking in sheer delight at their performance.

The Great Crested Grebe's water courtship only lasts for a few weeks. Soon the birds revert to the more sexual part of their pair-bonding, in which the displays take place out of water on a platform, usually in a more private setting than the open water on which they delight their audience.

So, if you can, set aside a day in March or April to watch this treat for yourself. You may find yourself in an audience of one, since most people simply have no idea about the drama that takes place on almost every British lake at this time of year. Consider yourself privileged.

Surface tension in Coots

THE BLACK plumage of a Coot perfectly express-es its mood. And I don't mean a temporary mood, the kind you might sink into over some brief injustice or fleeting problem. I mean a permanent, irritable, thoroughly unpleasant mood that never goes away. At times we all wake up a trifle tetchy, but the Coot always acts as though it has slipped out of the wrong side of its roost-site.

It sounds irritable, too. It clucks and it squawks and it squeals, and when several Coots are being noisy at once they sound like a warring couple having a furious argument, with raised voices and smashing glasses. The very name "Coot" derives from a contact call that is so short and curt that it even sounds like an insult.

Even the Coot's only redeeming physical feature, the white "frontal shield" above its bill, is used aggressively. When Coots confront each other, they lower their heads and ruffle their neck feathers to better show off this white badge against its black background. Males have larger frontal shields than females, and some individuals are more impressively endowed than others, regardless of their sex. The frontal shield is a permanent badge of dominance.

Dominance and power, indeed, are important parts of Coot life. These waterbirds live in flocks outside the breeding season, and within this social unit they maintain a hierarchy that is constantly refined by bickering. Even when among their own kind Coots will assert their personal space by what is known as a "charging attack", which is really a very fast swim towards an opponent, with head lowered. Thus the best feeding sites are

A splattering attack.

hotly contested, invariably falling to the dominant birds. Some powerful individuals don't actually bother to feed themselves, but spend their days stealing from subordinates. It's really just a floating version of the City.

Things don't get any better in the breeding season; indeed, if anything, the Coot becomes even more bad-tempered. To be fair, many species of bird get pretty aggressive at this time of the year defending their territories; but somehow they seem to be less overt about it than Coots. A pond in the breeding season can become virtually a battleground.

They certainly quarrel in style. When a Coot violates another's territory and is foolish enough not to retreat immediately, the owner will mount what is known as a "splattering attack", which is like a turbo-charged version of a charging attack: the bird doesn't just swim towards its opponent, but runs over the water surface, fluttering its wings, with double the speed and double the commotion. And if the intruder is foolish enough to stand its ground, it will be physically attacked in an avian version of kickboxing. Facing each other, the birds grapple with their feet and peck with their bills. The idea – as, for example, in judo – is to unbalance the other bird. But, just to make things more unpleasant, they also hold it under the water. The dispute is settled when one bird retreats by diving down and away.

As bystanders we can find this quite amusing. Coots certainly don't look dignified when angry, and they are so portly and cumbersome that

their fights can be strangely entertaining – like a spar between two boxers who should have retired long ago. But sometimes their aggression can turn on a more vulnerable target: their youngsters.

Picking on chicks may in certain circumstances not be especially surprising. After all, if a chick from another brood wanders into a coot's territory and starts to cause trouble, it might understandably feel annoyed – like a human householder when a neighbour's urchin kicks a ball through the glass of their greenhouse. But while the householder might give a kid a clip round the ear (lawsuits permitting), the adult Coot, similarly aggrieved, takes the rascal's head in its bill, shakes it and pushes it underwater.

Trespassing chicks attacked in this way are in real danger and sometimes play dead to get away. But the Coot's own chicks have no answer to their parent's ire. And, upsettingly, there are occasions when Coots do indeed kill their own chicks, quite deliberately and violently, in the manner described above. So far, it is not known why they do this, but it might be that by killing off the weaker siblings they enable the stronger to feed when the food supply is dangerously low. It is better for them to bring up one well-fed chick than to risk losing their entire brood.

Nonetheless, infanticide is never pretty. And, let's face it, Coots aren't very pretty, either. Their world is very black indeed.

Coots frequently fight using their feet.

Introducing Britain's Flamingo

FLAMINGOES ARE exciting birds, but they are wimps when it comes to the weather – or at least, the European species is. It can just about tolerate the South of France, but shuns a damp, chilly climate like ours. So we are bereft of these pink, long-legged birds, which remain to us icons of the exotic and faraway.

But though we may not have any flamingos, we do at least have Shovelers. This portly duck waddles from side to side as it walks on its short legs, and swims with a permanent stoop, bill seemingly glued to the water surface. It is about as similar to a flamingo as is a cow to a kangaroo. But cows and kangaroos are both grazers. And, at least in terms of their feeding trade, Shoveler and flamingo also have a lot in common. Both are filter feeders; the Shoveler, indeed, is the most specialised avian exponent of this art in Britain.

Flamingos and Shovelers both feed by filling their bills with water that contains edible items in suspension, and then passing this water through a structure inside that traps any edible particles while allowing the water to escape. The precise details of this structure are different, but the principle is the same. It is a little like panning for precious metals, but the filter feeders sieve the water and then eat the gold.

The Shoveler's bill is something to behold. It is remarkably long for that of a duck, and it is swollen laterally at the tip. When the bird is feeding, the water passes in through the tip and fills the mouth. It is then expelled through the sides using the suction of the tongue, but cannot get out without passing through an interlocking grid of comb-like projections, which trap minute particles in the process. The projections are found around the edge of both the upper and lower

Shovelers often form circles when feeding.

mandible, so when the bill is closed they inter-mesh from above and below, a little like teeth.

This filter feeding system is ideal for catching the small planktonic crustaceans, such as shrimps, minute molluscs and insect larvae, on which the Shoveler subsists. It does also occasionally dive underwater and catch prey by opening and closing the bill, but filtering remains its prime method of feeding.

Of course, feeding is most productive where the water is essentially a soup of edible items. Shallow water over a highly productive, muddy bottom is best, especially where it is close to thick surrounding vegetation. Here the briefest stirring of the goo will bring up enough food to keep a Shoveler occupied for some considerable time. Indeed, Shovelers have been observed feeding over a single spot for an hour and a half, going round and round, paddling their feet madly to agitate the mud like a toddler at the beach.

Agitating your own water, however, is quite hard work, so Shovelers commonly join forces to feed together. Filtering is a lot easier when you are swimming at another bird's feet, since the individual in front of you is effectively kicking the mud straight up your bill. So these portly ducks are often seen swimming in a circle of birds, like a conga line, each individual with its bill down on the water. Usually only a handful of individuals make up this formation, but you might sometimes see up to a hundred involved. And a ring of a hundred Shovelers is certainly an impressive sight.

Even more impressive, perhaps, than a flock of flamingos.

MARSHLAND

Bogged and clogged

MARSHES ARE atmospheric and mysterious places, their permanently waterlogged ground making it difficult and even dangerous for people to penetrate into their heart. Indeed, they would be shallow lakes were it not for the copious plant growth that creates a mini-forest over the water. This vegetation clogs the ground with stems, further protecting the marsh's inner core. To us, therefore, the marsh and its special birds remain out of reach, something we can only observe from a distance, on the margins. Our contact with marshland birds tends to be the sum of glimpses and shapes only hinted at.

IF YOU visit a marsh in winter, you will need to work hard to see your birds. There are several reasons for this. The most obvious is that there are not many birds to be seen: the species list is limited to a few specialists. Marshes tend to comprise quite a small range of plant species, and most offer little more than stems or narrow leaves, and have a restricted invertebrate population. Another reason is that any sort of windy weather – hardly the most unusual conditions in winter – can make a marsh almost unworkable, with the swaying of reeds and the ruffling of waves keeping the birds down. Yet another reason is that marsh birds are secretive; in

Previous spread: A Bittern keeps a low profile, while Reed Buntings show off on the reed tops.

Right: By pointing its head up, the Bittern enhances its camouflage in the reedbeds.

fact, they're more or less paranoid. Their shy, undemonstrative nature and cryptic camouflage plumage can defy the efforts of even the most patient and dedicated birdwatcher to find them.

Perhaps the most extreme example of camouflage among marsh birds is shown by one of our rarest birds in any habitat, the Bittern. This bird belongs to the same family as the familiar Grey Heron, and is not very much smaller; yet it is so extraordinarily well camouflaged that, despite its size, you simply never come across it. More than that: I have been within four yards of a Bittern and been quite unable to see it, even when I knew exactly where it was. The plumage matches the colour of dead winter reeds perfectly, and the speckles and striations mimic the haphazard shadows and stems of this plant arranged in their largely vertical way. To complement its camouflage, the Bittern moves very slowly and methodically, rather like a huge praying mantis. And, as a party trick, it can assume a vertical posture when alarmed, body rigid and head pointing skywards, and sway along with the reed stems. So, clearly, this is one bird that does not want to be seen.

Bitterns are also famously fussy in choosing their habitat – like pampered celebrities checking into a new hotel. For a start, no breeding Bittern

would think of occupying a reedbed of less than 20 hectares: there simply wouldn't be enough food to support it. Furthermore, Bitterns demand permanent water below their reeds of a depth of at least 10–25cm, and they do not appreciate much fluctuation in that level. The water must be fresh, not brackish, despite the fact that reeds often occur in saline conditions, and every suitable site must offer a broad range of both old and new reed growth. Finally, it is essential that there are channels of open water continually available within the reedbed. Bitterns feed primarily on fish such as eel and rudd, and in order to stalk them, they like to manoeuvre along such channels under cover of waterside vegetation. All in all, the Bittern's demands are so exacting that it is hanging by a thread as a breeding bird in Britain, where very few marshes are large enough to meet all its requirements.

Nevertheless, Bitterns are among the few birds found in the reedbed in the middle of winter. With their specialised plumage and feeding technique, they cannot occur anywhere else at any time. And although our breeding population is tiny, quite healthy numbers visit us from the Continent in severe winters, when Britain offers a temporary refuge from the harsher weather and frozen marshes over there. Then, just occasionally, we might get a chance to see one.

British Rail

Another bird that flourishes in Britain's reedbeds in the winter is the Water Rail. This bird is a relative of the Coot and Moorhen, those dark duck-like birds that swim about in rivers and lakes, and it often shares the dense waterside vegetation with the latter. The Water Rail carries some notable adaptations for coping with its habitat. It is primarily a terrestrial feeder, running through the forest of vertical stems in a marsh, and picking and probing for a variety of wetland animals, including snails, beetles and even Water Voles. To get around in such a congested habitat, the Water Rail has a specially flattened body that enables it to squeeze, cat-like, between the close-set stems. It also has very long toes, which not only allow it to cling to what relatively firm surfaces there might be, but also help to distribute its weight over a wide area, preventing it from sinking into the mud or mats of dead vegetation. All in all, no matter how hard you might try to run after a Water Rail, you'll never catch one.

Water Rails abound in the right habitat in winter. Their numbers in the UK, like those of the Bittern, are swollen by relatively large influxes of

immigrants from colder parts of Europe, and there is also a healthy breeding population here. You might be surprised to read that they are common, since many birdwatchers, even quite experienced ones, have never seen one, and the general public, by and large, have never heard of the Water Rail.

Huge feet and a thin body allow the Water Rail to scamper over swampy ground.

Yet, like the Bittern, it is a very secretive species, well camouflaged and extraordinarily furtive. Your best chance of seeing one is to place yourself in a bird hide and watch the muddy base of a reedbed, especially at dusk and dawn.

The reason for the reticence of the Bittern and Water Rail to show themselves is not immediately obvious. We can appreciate that marshes and reedbeds are difficult places in which to watch birds, and this might explain why we see so few of them. But it's hard not to also conclude that these birds are keeping their heads down for another reason: perhaps because reedbeds are very dangerous places.

The most specialised predator of this habitat is the Marsh Harrier, which uses a hunting strategy known as quartering to flush and catch its prey. This involves simply flying low and slowly over the marsh, keeping ear and eye out for any movement. Quartering harriers are very thorough in their reconnaissance, and can creep up upon their victims virtually silently. Prey animals that feel the breeze from the predator's wings in their hiding places, often lose their nerve and try to dash for safety. It's a fatal error. The danger from these birds must be so acute that it explains why most denizens of reedbeds have become so cryptic and unobtrusive.

Putting on the stones

Another species that can be found in reedbeds all year round is the Bearded Tit. This is a peculiar little bird with a thin body and long tail, not closely related to any other species in Britain. In fact its name is not very helpful: this bird is certainly not a tit – its bill is very different in shape and it builds its nest in the open rather than in a hole; neither does it have a beard, only a thin black moustache. An alternative name, albeit a less catchy one, is Bearded Reedling.

Whatever you call them, these odd little birds are totally dependent on reedbeds, going around in groups and nesting colonially. Though quite tricky to see, because they often feed out of sight, they are not as shy as Bitterns or Water Rails. But they are no less adapted for marshland life, having plumage that is easily lost among the dappled yellows and browns of mature reed stems, and strong, acrobats' feet that enable them to cling to their swaying, vertical perches. The long tail acts as a counterbalance for a life of swinging about on moving stems, much like the legs of a human trapeze artist.

The Bearded Tit is confined to reedbeds all year round. In the breeding season it is insectivorous, and often clings to the lowest point of stems where it grabs midges and other insects from the water's surface. It also

This Bearded Tit is taking reed seeds from the icy surface.

takes its food by racing up stems and jumping and flying from one to the other, often doing the splits between them. In the autumn and winter, however, as the marsh's insect supplies decline, it makes a dramatic shift in diet; for months it will now depend on the seeds of reeds, and nothing else. At this time you will most often see Bearded Tits on the soft, tufted flowerheads, hanging upside down just like true tits as they find sustenance by running their mandibles through the flowing locks of inflorescence. Later in the season, as the seeds fall, they turn to feeding on the ground, where they scratch at the soil with their feet, like chickens – revealing how different they are from true tits.

The shift from insect feeding to seed foraging has profound implications for the Bearded Tit's digestive system. In order to switch from easily processed, soft flesh to hard seeds, there is a great strengthening of the muscle tissue surrounding the stomach and intestine walls, with the result that these organs weigh twice as much in the winter as in the summer. During winter the birds also ingest large numbers (up to 400) of minute stones, which add bite to the grinding process of the stomach. How the bloated beardies must relish trim spring! Their winter weight is the price of adaptation to a very limited foodstuff in a limited habitat.

Spring surprises

A visit to a reedbed in early spring won't necessarily yield more bird sightings than in the dead of winter, but it will certainly be a much noisier place. One difficulty faced by birds living in dense marshy vegetation is that they cannot easily communicate with each other by sight, as

The handsome male Reed Bunting utters its staccato "Three…blind…mice" song from the reed-tops.

many birds do and take for granted. Thus marsh birds make loud sounds that carry their message far through the habitat. In early February breeding Bitterns begin to utter the lowest-pitched of all known British bird sounds, a deep booming grunt likened to the sound of a person blowing briefly over the rim of a glass bottle. This atmospheric sound can travel for 2km on a still day, and it is critical for Bittern communication because every "boom" is different and individually recognisable. Therefore the territorial males – which, incidentally, can attract and pair with up to five females concurrently in a season – are able to insult each other ritually from a safe distance.

Alongside the booming, the Water Rail makes a remarkable sound of its own. It is a sequence of loud grunts and squeals that has been likened to the noise of a piglet being throttled; and much as you might object to or scoff at this comparison, it rings true when you hear it. The Water Rail's colleague, the Moorhen, also adds its own element to the early spring chorus, with its usual disapproving squeaks and clucks, seemingly always uttered in surprise. On the watery parts of the marsh Teals will be displaying, the males making soft, very persistent calls like slightly muted cowbells, the females uttering a quiet, hoarse quack as if they had a frog in their throat – quite unlike the loud, nagging, belly-laugh sequence of the female Mallard, another common sound at this time of year. If you add the occasional *"ping"* from Bearded Tits, and the rhythmic, broken "Three…blind…mice" from a Reed Bunting perched on a spray of vegetation, the marshland soundscape can be surprisingly strong and varied, even in the midst of grinding cold.

With the coming of the breeding season, though, there is a profound change in the marsh. The new growth of reed is green and lush, and provides food for a significantly increased invertebrate population. Alongside the reed, many other

Reed Warblers have strong legs and feet for holding on to vertical reed stems.

plants flourish and flower, everything from the brilliant buttercup-yellow of irises to the shy blue of forget-me-nots and the powdery white of bog-bean and water-dropwort. Suddenly the marsh is attractive to many more species, besides its resident stalwarts, as though it had undergone a complete fashion makeover from tired winter rags to fresh spring wardrobe.

Among the birds drawn to this new-look habitat are several migrants, including two particularly perky characters, the Reed Warbler and the Sedge Warbler. Both are small and brown and, in common with the marshland trend, they have big voices, dominating the summer chorus with their chattering and chuntering. At first you wonder how two species that are evidently so similar can occur in the same habitat without competing against one another, but careful study has thrown light on their subtly different ecology. The Reed Warbler is confined as a breeding bird to stands of the Common Reed, *Phragmites*, usually those growing out of shallow water. It constructs its highly unusual nest amidst these vertical columns, by which the nest is also supported. This is usually placed about 50cm above the water and, not surprisingly, is pretty safe from any predators that don't like getting their feet wet. An ideal stand for Reed Warblers is at least 1.2m tall, with a stem density of at least 40 per square metre. Any less, and the nest is difficult to support.

The Sedge Warbler, on the other hand, is not confined to reedbeds at all, but is really a bird of the marshland fringes. On the landward side of a bed of reeds there is often a rich community of plants, including sedges and rushes and, in the drier areas, stands of bramble and small bushes. Here the Sedge Warbler builds a much more conventional nest than that of its relatives – a simple cup placed in thick vegetation over dry land. Without its dependence upon a particular plant, it inhabits larger territories than the Reed Warbler and is

sometimes found well away from any water.

The two species also differ in their feeding. Sedge Warblers tend to find most of their insect food close to the ground, and specialise on slower-moving prey than that favoured by the Reed Warbler. In fact, they often do much of their foraging in the early morning, when the insects are still cold and half-asleep. Reed Warblers, on the other hand, usually zip around towards the middle and top of the vegetation, dashing to and fro to catch turbo-charged insects, often snatching them on a jump between reeds – like Tarzan grabbing fruit on his way from tree to tree.

Bedding down

At the end of the breeding season, when the insect life of the marsh once again begins to diminish, some birds find a whole new use for reedbeds – as roosting sites. Plants growing out of water are, of course, unusually safe places to sleep, because they not only keep ground-based predators, such as people, well out of the way, but also the splashing of a prowling carnivore and its disturbance of the stems makes a stealthy approach almost impossible. At any rate, plenty of birds are drawn to reedbeds at night and they may come here from autumn onwards. Swallows utilise them during their slow initial migration in August and September, stopping over on marshes as often as

they can while moving south. Sand Martins may join them, both birds taking advantage of the inevitable supplies of midges and other marsh-land insects that are present nearby on shallow pools. Pied and Yellow Wagtails also use the vertical stems for security. Closely packed reed stems presumably also provide some shelter from the wind.

The most spectacular roosting concentrations to be found in reedbeds are those of a familiar garden bird, the Starling. These talkative avian wide-boys are better known for their habit of roosting on buildings in city centres, but reedbeds are a more natural site, with a history of use that predates cities by thousands of years. In many areas the Starlings always choose reedbeds over other potential roosting habitats.

Indeed, arguably the single most impressive gathering of birds anywhere in Britain at any time of year occurs in reedbeds. In the Somerset Levels, one single large reedbed currently provides a roosting site for up to eight million birds every night between November and January. Most of these are visitors from the continent, escaping the same conditions that bring Bitterns and Water Rails here, too. In a habitat that is generally quite impoverished for birds, it is curious that such a phenomenon, perhaps the most spectacular of all, should occur here.

Reedbeds make safe places for roosting – these are Starlings.

The high-flyers

HAVE YOU ever watched a bird setting out on its migration? Probably not: it's not an easy event to witness. You might just catch some geese or ducks taking off from a lake or estuary and flying far away over the horizon, but you would be hard pressed to see a smaller bird doing the same, metaphorically locking up and disappearing down the street. Birds such as Flycatchers or Willow Warblers are very discreet about it, leaving alone and at night. It is as if, somehow, the departure was a slightly sacrosanct event, requiring privacy and concealment. After all, a migration is a huge undertaking, albeit with humble beginnings, so perhaps birds are daunted by it and prefer to leave without ceremony.

One bird of the reedbeds, however, makes a real song and dance about its departure. The Bearded Tit is a social species, and you could almost say that it throws a leaving party in honour of those that are going. This exodus is announced in advance, and then the travellers leave during quite a bash. Nobody knows why Bearded Tits do this, and no other small bird in Britain carries on remotely like it. The Bearded Tit is a rather odd bird, with odd colours and odd habits, but this, perhaps, is its oddest quirk of all.

It takes until late September for the first "evictions" to occur. All the adults and first-year birds have moulted into fresh plumage and gathered into flocks. Only now does the productivity of the breeding season just gone become apparent to all, and the birds can monitor whether resources are going to be strained in the winter to come. If the crop of reed seeds is not up to it, some birds will have to go. In lean years of low breeding productivity and decent seed production there may be no migration at all, but more usually some birds must leave their colony to relieve the pressure on their home marsh. Reedbeds are a finite resource, and can only support a limited number of individuals. Thus, in most autumns, there is a call for birds to move away.

This call takes an extraordinary form, expressed in a unique social display known as "high-flying". At any time of day, but always on still, sunny days, the display is triggered when one bird gives a sort of rallying call from within the reedbed. This is similar to the usual Bearded Tit call, a sort of "*pching*" sounding like a mini cash register, but louder. At once a party of birds, sometimes as many as 25, flies straight up into the air on whirring wings, the members calling excitedly like a group of schoolchildren. They may reach a height of 100m, and often disappear from sight. But you will usually still be able to hear them as they fly towards the perimeter of their home reedbed and then, as quickly as they rose, plummet back to earth and fall silent – except for the odd quiet contact call. Sometimes, by mistake, they will land outside the reedbed and settle on a field, or even on a bush, whereupon they soon realise their mistake and zoom sheepishly back to the marsh, tails trailing.

What is so striking about this display is that the birds seem so completely ill-equipped for it. You normally see Bearded Tits flying just above the reed tops, their short wings whirring so desperately fast that it seems, at any time, that they might stall, fall and crash into a stem. Their tail seems to impede them, prompting at least one observer to have likened their erratic progress to that of a miniature Pheasant. Yet, when high-

Bearded Tits travel by day so that they can spot wetlands below.

flying, these birds are making spectacular ascents and descents worthy of a Swift or Peregrine Falcon. It seems that they are showing off beyond their means, and that – like Icarus – some mishap is bound to befall them. Surely they must see the folly of their showboating? We may never see pigs fly, but at least we can watch Bearded Tits.

From about the third week of September, some of these high-flying displays reach a slightly different conclusion. It confirms that the previous high jinks have just been a prelude to the more serious undertaking of migratory dispersal. At the peak of the ascent, some birds peel away from the rest of their group and, instead of plummeting down, continue flying at high altitude, moving away from their home reedbed towards a destination that is probably unknown to them. Most British Bearded Tits seem to move south-west, but not all do so, and it might be that the birds are dispersing randomly. They do not fly particularly high and, because they also move by day, it is likely that they are looking out as they go for a new place to spend the winter. It's not hard to imagine that, from their modest height above the ground, they can easily spot the distinctive form of a reedbed.

You might expect these parties to be made up mainly of juvenile birds but, interestingly, adults travel too. The precise composition of the "erupting" groups is one of the many mysteries of Bearded Tit behaviour. Curiously, there is plenty of evidence that birds tend to travel in pairs and even in small flocks. If so, the even sex ratio could ensure that, should the travellers find a highly promising reedbed, they have the wherewithal to form a new colony.

Rarely, however, do the travellers embark on such a grand mission. More usually, it seems, they simply spread out, find themselves smaller stands of reeds and pass the winter there, before returning to their home marsh in the early spring. They have served their time away from the colony, releasing pressure upon the winter reedbed, and now they can fill in for those birds that have died or have not returned. At any rate, a reedbed is more productive in the summer, and is able to support more Bearded Tits.

This time, though, there is no fanfare. The return of the high-flyers is muted and subdued. They melt into the reeds and keep a low profile until the autumn air calls them skywards again.

The Sedge Warbler's secret ingredient

THE VISITS of several of our reedbed birds are somewhat brief, summer flings. And so it is with a spirited, small brown bird called the Sedge Warbler.

This sprite arrives in April, whereupon the males sing zestfully all day long, occasionally punctuating their perched performances with brief flights into the air for that little bit of extra choreographic flair. Once paired, however, they fall silent and the Sedge Warbler, having been a dominantly noisy feature of the water margins, disappears into the scrub to follow its breeding routine in comparative anonymity. It feeds mainly close to the ground, near the base of reeds and other plants of the water's edge, which means that it becomes very difficult to see when it falls silent. Only the Sedge Warbler's effervescence and inherent curiosity prevents it from becoming completely reclusive. If you remain within one's territory for long enough, a small face will probably soon peer out from behind a leaf and scold your intrusion.

By late summer, however, the Sedge Warblers have brought up their young and the gradually declining day length in July and August prompts them to plan their departure from Britain. Although it is only a few months since they arrived, breathless, with the whole summer in front of them, their inner migratory drive already has them restless for the wetlands of West Africa.

Meanwhile a very closely related bird has followed a similar course. The Reed Warbler arrives a little later in the season than the Sedge, and has to pack its programme into an even tighter schedule if it is to reproduce successfully. More strictly

The irrepressible Sedge Warbler is a perky, inquisitive bird.

birds of reedbeds than Sedge Warblers, and more apt to feed in the middle sections of the forest of stems, Reed Warblers are, on the whole, more noticeable. They sing for longer in the season, too, so that theirs is really the signature sound of the busy summer reedbed. The song sounds like a long series of variations on the theme of a fast hiccup, and, while most birds' refrains are quite clearly cut into phrases that are repeated, the Reed Warbler's is a non-stop, long-winded paragraph several pages long. Telephone a Reed Warbler at your peril – especially if you're paying the bill.

In late summer the Reed Warbler is also preparing for migration. Once it has left our country it is heading for a similar destination to the Sedge Warbler's, and it follows a broadly similar calendar, leaving at about the same time. One might expect that, being a close relative, it would undertake its migration in a strikingly similar manner. But this is not the case. The migrations of the Reed Warbler and the Sedge Warbler, though they cover the same ground, could scarcely follow more different strategies. And this is all to do with a secret dietary ingredient that propels the Sedge Warbler to its destination with all the vim of a spinach-fuelled Popeye.

Let me introduce you to a sort of wonder drug. Nobody knows what it is, and nobody knows what it does chemically, but it is undeniably found within the copious juices of a tiny insect known as the Plum-reed Aphid. This reddish-coloured bug is confined to reedbeds, hence its name; but some reedbeds have very many more of them than others, and their appearance is somewhat unpredictable. Marshes in southern England often have good stocks; in other years, if a Sedge Warbler truly wishes to gorge itself, it travels to Northern France. The fact is that, in late July and August, Sedge Warblers seek out high densities of these insects, wherever they may be. And, for several weeks, they consume huge numbers of them.

Meanwhile Reed Warblers, while not entirely shunning Plum-reed Aphids, do not seek them in the same single-minded way. They follow the feeding regime that is typical of small migrant birds in general, taking in a broad diet which includes some fruit in the form of berries, and plenty of invertebrates of various kinds. They feed constantly throughout the day, and put on their migratory fuel in the form of fat. In fact, small birds like these can double their body weight from 10g to 20g in just a few weeks before departure. The invertebrate bodies provide the vital protein that the travellers need, but do not imbue them with any special migratory powers.

The Reed Warbler's migration is, in fact, rather a ponderous one. It progresses in small legs of just a few tens of kilometres, at least at the beginning,

Like spinach to Popeye…

and is punctuated by many breaks. The birds fly during the night, setting off just after sunset, and sometimes travel for only a few hours before stopping to rest. As they reach the Mediterranean and North Africa, however, the legs of their journey grow longer and they probably overfly the Sahara Desert in a single burst. But this marathon may not be attempted until several weeks into the migratory journey.

Sedge Warblers, on the other hand, are fuelled by their wonder drug and approach their task in a far more vigorous way. Plum-full of aphids, they take off from Northern Europe with a following wind and fly high into the sky. They continue for the whole night and also for the next day; when night falls again they are still flying, and they pass over south-west Europe without once touching down. In fact, so far as is known, Sedge Warblers take their whole journey in a single stretch. For three days and three nights they carry on flying, and by the time they reach their West African wintering grounds they have covered about 4,000km. Exhausted, they flutter down into a very different kind of landscape from the one in which they enjoyed their last meal.

We tend to hear so much about the wonders of migration that there is a danger we might grow blasé about the remarkable feats of migrant birds. Many of the most famous stories are about navigation, or about the gauntlet of obstacles and perils that birds must run on their journeys. But perhaps the most extraordinary aspect of migration is in its physiology: what are the internal processes that prepare, propel and guide birds along their way? Down at the chemical level the engine room of bird travel has a few stories of its own to tell. And one of its most intriguing is the secret ingredient that powers 20g of bird on 70–90 hours of non-stop flight.

Service with style

Groom service – a male Marsh Harrier (top) delivers food to its mate in mid-air.

IF YOU are ever treated to the sight of a Marsh Harrier display flight, you'll no doubt be blown away by its acrobatic audacity. The male flies up to a great height, plunges down at high speed, then uses his momentum to sweep up again and repeat the manoeuvre. And just to add a seasoning of extra bravura, his progress along this course is never straight. The bird makes spectacular spins about its axis, quivers its wings, and often gives the intoxicating impression of being completely out of control, especially while plummeting towards the ground. Every time the male spins around, the female is invited to appreciate his fine patchwork plumage of black, brown and silver-grey. This sky-dance, as it is appropriately called, may continue above the marsh for hours on end on warm, still days from March until June.

It's a highly impressive sight, but you sometimes get the impression that behind the showmanship there is little genuine substance. You might even wonder whether, except for its entertainment value, there is any real point in a plummeting harrier. After all, many species of birds are great displayers, but lousy partners and parents. Can the same be said for the Marsh Harrier?

You'll be pleased to know, and perhaps a little surprised, that this is not the case at all. The male Marsh Harrier doesn't just impress at the beginning of a relationship: he continues to impress throughout. As well as continuing with his "extreme displaying" throughout the season, to the beguilement of his female, he is also an excellent provider for both his mate and his chicks. He seems, overall, to be a bird of considerable substance. In fact, he is one of the hardest-working birds of prey in the world.

The Marsh Harrier's true labour begins in May, when the female begins to build the nest. At this time she becomes too busy with important nuptial tasks to take the time to feed herself, and responsibility for her entire provision is passed to the male. Dutifully, he quarters the reedbeds and adjacent farmland with redoubled effort, and catches enough birds or small mammals to satisfy both his own needs and those of his mate.

It's not long, though, before the female's needs increase. Nest-building is a relatively undemanding process, not requiring vast reserves of strength, but egg-laying, her next task, is exhausting and drains her reserves of energy. Her appetite therefore becomes greater, and the number of trips made over the reed-tops increases for the male. This continues while the female produces between three and six eggs. During egg-laying, she remains on the nest for much of the day, entirely dependent upon the male's offerings. He has now been providing food for both of them for about a month. It is worth remembering, too, that his trips are not like our supermarket runs, where we simply pick up what we need from the shelves. The male has to catch prey that hides, flees and generally does its best to avoid being eaten. His hard work involves guile and technique, as well as sweat.

Remarkably, though, his workload soon increases still further, as the eggs begin to hatch. If the whole clutch is healthy and fertile, and there are therefore six new mouths to feed, he must provide for them all. The female, meanwhile, must brood the chicks, keeping them warm, sheltered and protected. For the moment she cannot leave them, as they are unable to regulate their own body temperature. Instead, she must depend, as ever, upon the male's extraordinary efforts.

At last, some four to ten days after the last chick hatches, the male gets some relief. The chicks can look after themselves a little more and, for the first time in sixty days, he is no longer hunting for them alone. The commanding figure of the dark-clad female is now a regular sight above the reeds. The male cannot afford to slacken off – the chicks are only getting bigger and more demanding – but at least his workload is no longer increasing. Two harriers now terrorise the marshland bird community.

One might expect, during the unrelenting toil of providing for his family, that the male might fray around the edges a little and cut a few corners. He might, for example, forget the flourish and high-spirits of his displaying and pairing days and simply drop the food parcels with a yawn and a sigh. Yet, remarkably, he does not, at least not until the young have hatched. Every time he feeds the female he does so in great style, making the food-pass of the Marsh Harrier one of the great sights of marshland birding.

Where there are birds of prey there is blood. The Marsh Harrier has a varied diet of marshland creatures.

It goes like this. Each time the male arrives with a prey item, he gives out a wild mewing call while still some distance from the nest – a few doors down the street, so to speak. Upon hearing this, the female takes off and begins to fly on her mate's coat-tails, just below and behind him, in slow pursuit. At this point the male, with his legs dangling down, drops the gift into the air, whereupon the female dexterously catches it in her talons. Marsh Harriers have very long legs, and this sort of slip fielding comes naturally to them. Sometimes, especially when dealing with smaller items, the female flips over in mid-air and presents her talons to the male while upside down. The meal is passed talon-to-talon, in an act of balletic grace and flourish.

Amidst the hard labour of a Marsh Harrier breeding season, this display rises above the drudgery. It is truly service with style.

RUNNING WATER

Current affairs

RIVERS ARE unique in that they lead several "lives" at the same time. They have a youth, in which they are all fast streams and boiling rapids. Meanwhile, further downstream, they meander through the moderation of middle age. And at their mouth, they are constantly meeting their slow and expansive end. At each stage their character is dramatically different and so, as a result, is their birdlife: the inhabitants of the fast streams are quite different from those of the slower bends. Furthermore, the surrounding countryside is also very different at each of these stages. It is misleading, therefore, to consider a river as a single habitat: it is an amalgam of many.

BIRDS MAKE use of rivers at all their stages and in many different ways. Some species are found on rushing streams; others only in the slower, wider sections. Some immerse themselves fully in the water; others remain on the fringes. Some are year-round occupants of the flowing water; others simply use the floodlands created when the river bursts its banks in winter. A few, indeed, may resort to swimming on the river only when all the nearby lakes and ponds are frozen. Yet, over the course of a year, many birds find themselves dependent on moving freshwater in one way or another.

It is only near the source of a river that you will find a unique set of birds that occurs commonly nowhere else. Here the foaming rapids form a special habitat that requires specialist adaptations for survival. Further downstream, where the current is less wild, the waters can support more general wetland birds, such as Mallards and Moorhens. Swans are often found in rivers, but they also occur on freshwater lakes and in marshes; even Kingfishers, so emblematic of flowing water, are also quite at home by lakes and ponds, especially in winter. But the birds of the rapids are different: they are tied to this demanding habitat, and consequently are rather less well-known characters than those others so familiar to anglers and towpath-users.

Above: Eating seeds make you thirsty, so these Siskins are grateful to live by the riverside.

Taming the torrent

The supreme bird of the torrents is the Dipper. This bird, which looks like a big, plump Wren wearing a white bib, lives only along fast-flowing streams, where it swims in and under the water, paddles in the shallows and perches on rocks. Its favourite food is underwater insect larvae, which abound in these highly oxygenated rushing waters. They aren't easy to get at, though, and the Dipper has to battle the current daily as it searches the slippery rocks and churning stream-bed. Although it looks a portly bird, it is supremely streamlined underwater, and can easily immerse itself without being swept away. Research has shown that the Dipper does well in streams that flow swiftly down gradients, which offer plenty of rocks, pools, shallows and riffles where it can forage for food. Such streams also provide nest sites in streamside crevices – a Dipper's nest is often soaked in permanent spray. Suitable streams also need to be clear and relatively free of pollutants, which would soon wipe out the invertebrate population. Despite its apparent fussiness, however, the Dipper is still quite a widespread bird in Northern and Western Britain.

Only one other species regularly immerses itself in these rushing waters, and that is the Goosander. This is a large duck that feeds by chasing and catching fast-swimming fish, including trout and salmon – a habit that hardly endears it to the anglers who share its waters. The Goosander's strong webbed feet are set well back on its body, giving it efficient and powerful propulsion, and this helps it to deal with the current, as well as catch its tricky prey. Goosanders usually feed in the deeper stretches of river, and nest in large tree-holes beside the water. They have special bills that are lined with sharp serrations, enabling the birds to grip their slippery prey.

Two other species are highly characteristic of the upper reaches of rivers, but neither is a swimmer. Instead, they perch on rocks, walk along the water's edge and paddle in the shallows, usually getting nothing more than their feet wet. Interestingly, the two are completely unrelated: the Grey Wagtail is a small perching bird that feeds by the river, but frequently perches on overhanging branches to sing; the Common Sandpiper is a wading bird with a long bill that it uses to pick insects off rocks and other surfaces. Both may also be found in other habitats, such as along lakeshores, but they are most at home in fast-flowing upland waters, with their abundant supply of streamside insects.

Although the Common Sandpiper is, on the whole, a non-swimmer, there are circumstances in which it will enter the water – notably when it is fleeing for its life. On such occasions the Sandpiper will, as is its custom, fly very low over the water, with odd, flickering wing-beats that never seem to rise above the horizontal. But should the danger get too close it will simply dive in and disappear, using its wings as paddles to swim ashore when the coast is clear.

Always found near water, the Grey Wagtail fields insects from the riverside mud and rocks.

The birds that feed in the shallows share one peculiar characteristic: they all dip their bodies up and down in a rhythmic motion. In the case of wagtails the habit is well-known enough to have given them their name: they wag their rear ends incessantly. But the Common Sandpiper does it, too – and in perhaps an even more exaggerated, bobbing fashion. For its part the Dipper doesn't wag its rear end, but instead flexes its legs so that it, too, rocks up and down, like a cartoon policeman. It cannot be coincidence that all these foragers of the shallows are also bobbers, but explaining the habit is much more difficult. Various theories have been put forward, but the one with the most credence suggests that the bobbing, or "teetering", probably makes the birds more noticeable to their peers or rivals should the latter land nearby. It thus serves as a form of communication and territorial proclamation. The fast-flowing river habitat is a noisy one, and it is clearly useful to be able to communicate in this non-verbal, and also continuous way.

The Dipper also blinks. All birds have eyelids but in the majority of species you'd never notice them because they are dull in colour. Those of the Dipper, however, are white and very obvious. When two rival Dippers meet their rate of blinking (as well as dipping) increases, so this, too, is clearly a form of silent communication in a noisy world.

Downstream

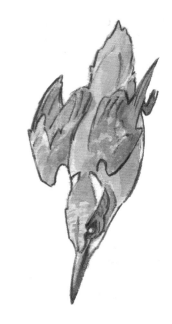

Once a river leaves behind the turbulence of its youth for the more gentle gradients and currents of middle age, the cast of characters changes radically. The birds of the torrents are left behind, to be replaced by a much greater number and variety of other river users. The water here is deeper and calmer than in the uplands, allowing a higher proportion of birds to make a living by swimming, dabbling or diving. Thus the ubiquitous Mallard soon makes an appearance, followed by the Moorhen and the Little Grebe. Mallards feed in all sorts of ways, including sieving food from the water surface. Moorhens depends on good quality emergent vegetation, where they tiptoe after snails and other small invertebrates, picking them from leaves, stems and lily-pads. Little Grebes stick to quiet backwaters, where they make short dives for aquatic insects and their larvae, and chase after small fish. If danger threatens, Little Grebes head for the emergent vegetation and can submerge all but their heads, becoming almost impossible to see.

Perhaps the best known of all the river inhabitants, however, is a non-swimmer, the Kingfisher. In common with the Little Grebe it cannot cope with turbulent water, so it tends to be scarce in the upper reaches of rivers. This aversion to swift currents is perfectly logical: not only is the Kingfisher a small plunge-diver that would risk being swept away in rough water, but the state of such water, churned up and glinting with light, makes it much more difficult to spy fishes through the surface from above. The Kingfisher relies completely on its ability to work in two media: first spotting food from a perch in the open air, and then snapping it up under the water. If it cannot see the fish, it naturally cannot catch them.

The Kingfisher's ability to catch fish by diving into the water is greatly aided by some special adaptations to its eyesight. For one thing, its eyes have exceptional colour vision, enabling the bird to make out every conceivable hue and nuance on the water surface and therefore to detect the outline of fishes. Secondly, its eyes are positioned in such a way that, unusually, it has both excellent all-round vision and the ability to focus very closely on a target. When its head is tilted at an angle of about 60° to the water, a slight lifting will bring in its all-round vision to scan for prey. A slight lowering, however, will cause the fields of view of the two eyes to overlap more, creating the "binocular vision" that allows accurate judgement of distance and enables the bird to target its prey with precision.

Kingfishers make use of many parts of the

A Kingfisher meets its reflection and a fish is snapped up.

river, including the shallows, the deeps and the waterside vegetation. And during the breeding season they also use the banks, digging a burrow a metre or so into the soft sand to make a safe, secure nest-hole. In this habit they are not alone. Sand Martins also make holes in riverbanks, which they too dig out with their feet, a hard graft for a small bird, and their burrows are not so different in length from those of the Kingfisher. This, though, is where the resemblance ends. Sand Martins are sociable, whereas Kingfishers are strictly territorial. Sand Martins often change breeding sites from one year to another, while

Kingfishers stay put. And as a far cry indeed from a diet of fish, Sand Martins feed on flying insects that they snatch in mid-air, or sometimes just above the water surface.

Fierce rivals

Towards the end of its journey to the sea, a river often slows down, allowing its banks to widen still further. This increases the opportunities for the birds that feed in open stretches of water, and the river may now play host to a Great Crested Grebe for the first time, or a Tufted Duck, or Coots. These species are all primarily lake birds, but wider rivers are little more than moving lakes, anyway, so the large grebes hunt for fast-swimming fishes, the Tufted Duck plies the bottom for shellfish and the Coots dive down to snatch vegetation, just as they all do on their still-water strongholds.

A more confirmed river bird is the Mute Swan – although it is not confined to them. One important characteristic it shares with other true river birds is the holding of linear territories, and its extremely aggressive defence of them. If you walk along a suitable river in the spring, you are bound to come across Mute Swan nests from time to time, but will notice that they are never very close together, and the male of each pair, at least, tends to maintain an intimidating presence along its own stretch. We've all seen what rivals can do when they meet: one male drives away an interloper with an intense threat display, full of hissing, lunging and boiling water. The combatants often come to blows, snapping at each other with their bills and apparently attempting to drown their opponent. They rarely achieve this, but injuries are common, and – in severe cases – may add up to a long, drawn-out death sentence.

Most of us know the Mute Swan's aggression well, and the bird is indeed notorious: male swans, acting in a red mist of testosterone, often attack canoeists and dogs. But what is not widely known is that the phenomenon of the linear territory seems to be a recipe for tension: it seems that birds find it harder to squeeze into the gaps between river boundaries than into the more three-dimensional structure of, say, a woodland. Species that you would not expect to be aggressive, such as wagtails and Kingfishers, frequently kill rivals in fights. Clearly, these birds feel the need to protect their own stretch of river jealously in order to secure inviolable territories for feeding or breeding.

This is a rather surprising phenomenon. It somehow doesn't seem right that birds inhabiting such a calming and soothing environment are actually characterised by fierce territorial aggression. Yet it is one of the few things shared by the disparate group of birds that occur along rivers.

Mute Swans often fight, but these conflicts rarely result in injury.

Kingfisher carousels

Youthful democracy – young Kingfishers are fed in rotation.

EQUALITY IS not a word you normally associate with birds. All birds are not created equal. Some are superior to others, and these tend to survive at the expense of their inferiors. Even in the nest, young birds barely out of the egg fight one another for every offering of food. The stronger ones feed well and thrive; the weaker ones seldom live long enough to realise they are not equal.

But there are, surprisingly enough, a few places where equality reigns in the bird world. And, even more remarkably, one of these places exists along a river, that hotbed of territorial conflict. More amazingly still, it occurs within the domain of the Kingfisher, one of the most volatile of all river residents. The place of calm is in the Kingfisher's nest, where such a spirit of equality and diplomacy prevails that you might momentarily forget about the competitive world outside.

Kingfishers are productive birds, and regularly lay six or seven eggs. These are secreted away in a tunnel that the male digs into the sandy bank of a river, well above the water surface. The tunnel is, on average, 55cm long, and there is a large chamber at the end where all the incubation takes place. Despite the tunnel being so deep, it is usually horizontal, so the eggs and young are, by day, bathed in weak light from the outside world. Thus the parents can see what they are doing and, later on, the nestlings can tell when they are about to be fed.

Now, you might think that in such clearly visible surroundings the visit of a parent with a tasty fish might trigger something of a free-for-all. None of the youngsters could fail to know that food was imminent, and everything in their makeup would scream for immediate action – a bolt towards the parent and a grab for the fish. Yet this does not happen. Instead, young Kingfishers take their food in turns. Despite their tender age, the nestlings show a remarkable discipline, which ensures that the food is shared equally.

Throughout the early part of the brood's development, young Kingfishers remain sitting in a ring, with their bills pointing outward. The youngster whose turn it is to be fed makes sure that it is closest to the light coming in from outside, and when the parent enters the nest, this nestling is the only one that begs. It is duly presented with a fish, which it swallows. Once satisfied, it moves to one side, while the rest of the brood all shift around until the next bird is facing the light and duly becomes the next to be fed. This is just like a carousel slide projector, which rotates around the drum allowing each slide in turn to slip into the light and thus be projected onto the screen. And indeed, this unusual feeding arrangement is known as the carousel system.

What is most remarkable about this set-up is that the young accept it without complaint. They are not, as far as is known, tutored in the art of carousel feeding by the parents, nor coerced into it. The adults stay out of it, and simply feed the nearest bird each time they visit. Instead the scheme is self-regulating. Any individual that attempts to queue jump is pecked by the rest; there are even records of such miscreants literally being thrown to the back of the nest chamber. The young adopt their formation on pure instinct, and the system allows every bird to receive an equal share of food, provided that it is strong and alert enough to move into place when its turn comes.

The carousel system lasts for a couple of weeks or so and then, interestingly, everything changes. The young throw off their radial arrangement and adopt a so-called "roof-tile" pattern, facing the light in a formation that resembles those photos you see of winning football teams, with the players in front squatting and those at the back standing. This is more competitive than the carousel system, in that each chick will face the visiting adult and beg for food at the same time, and the adults must chose which mouth to fill. But it is still quite a disciplined and rigid arrangement. Finally, though, as the time of fledging approaches, all discipline breaks down in favour of the usual free-for-all seen among the nestlings of most other birds.

By the standards of most nestling feeding systems, the carousel system is astonishingly fair. In most birds, meritocracy rules among nestlings, ensuring that the most vigorous chicks get the most food, and are rewarded for their physical prowess with an enhanced chance of survival. Kingfishers, however, eschew this natural justice in favour of a chance for all.

The reasons for this may be hard to explain. But, in a world of incessant, throat-grabbing competition, it makes a pretty refreshing change.

The underwater songbird

IF YOUR garden Robin suddenly decided to jump into your pond and go for a swim, you'd probably be pretty surprised. Small brown song-birds just don't go in for that sort of thing. They take a bath from time to time, sitting self-consciously in the shallow water and ruffling their body feathers to get rid of dust and parasites, but that's about it. An aquatic lifestyle hardly suits them.

But there is one songbird that has embraced swimming as a way of life, and that is the Dipper. This is a bird of fast-flowing, well oxygenated rivers, where the powerful currents give even big, strong birds something to think about. Here the tiny Dipper lives and thrives, dividing its time between searching for food underwater and perching on damp, streamside rocks. It's tough making a living in this habitat, yet the Dipper spends its life dipping in and out of the turbulent water, as much as home as a toddler in a paddling-pool.

What is truly extraordinary about the Dipper is that it simply doesn't look like a waterbird. It doesn't, for example, have webbed feet, which is an immediate contravention of the first law of swimming. You'd also expect it to wear goggles, or at least have some obvious and unusual adaptation to its extreme way of life. But it doesn't. If you had a row of museum specimens before you and had to pick out the species most suited for an underwater life, it's unlikely you'd plump for the dipper.

That's not to say that Dippers don't have any adaptations, because they do; it's just that they're subtle ones. Perhaps the most important is the extremely dense plumage, which helps to insulate the Dippers against both the water and the cold. These feathers are highly waterproofed, being loaded with a high volume of water-resistant oil that the bird administers during constant preening sessions. The preen gland is unusually large for a bird this size, and the result is that, when a Dipper surfaces after a dive, the water flows off its back in the manner of the proverbial duck. Thus the Dipper has an effective barrier to prevent any water reaching its skin, and you could say, possibly stretching the point a little, that it wears a permanent dry-suit.

Another advantage of being clothed in dense feathers is that you become almost immune to cold. Dippers are hardy birds, existing in their chilly habitat throughout the winter. They

A Dipper at work in the shallows.

frequently dive under ice, and on the continent they have been observed foraging unconcerned in temperatures of up to –45°C. Britain's climate, one can safely conclude, is hardly a problem.

Other adaptations also help the Dipper meet the day-to-day challenges of the aquatic lifestyle. For example, it has a helpful flap of skin that covers its nose while underwater, preventing water from entering its nostrils. Its eyes have strong muscles controlling the iris, and it is thought that these help modify the lens to cope with the different refractive properties of the two mediums in which it lives, air and water. Dippers also have a high concentration of haemoglobin in their blood, which enables them to store more oxygen than other comparable birds, and thus fuel their relatively long dives. Their heartbeat rate drops rapidly as soon as they immerse, too, which helps to slow down their use of this precious oxygen. All in all, the Dipper's battery of internal adaptations is as unusual as its external characteristics are not.

It's all very well being adapted for your habitat, but how do Dippers actually work underwater? You may wear a suit to work in your office, but that doesn't give you management skills. The Dipper needs special foraging methods to cope with the turbulent current around it. Its main food – underwater insects, especially mayfly nymphs and caddis larvae – tends to be found on or

Placed behind a waterfall and protected by a sheet of water, this must be the most predator-proof nest in Britain!

underneath small pebbles or rocks, so it is essential for a Dipper to get to the riverbed in order to feed itself.

That's not as easy as it might sound. The Dipper, with all its portliness and waterproofing, is highly buoyant, and reaching the bottom at all, let alone through a fast-flowing current, is tricky. But the Dipper defies buoyancy by using its wings: it "flies" down and up underwater by flapping hard and angling its body accordingly. This requires a great deal of energy, and the Dipper has impressive wing-muscles with which to power itself. The wings are also rather short and stubby, thus favouring strength over finesse. So a foraging Dipper is constantly beating its wings, the power-stroke taking it down to where the food is richest. For up to thirty seconds a dive, the Dipper flaps to fight the physics of fast flowing water.

It was once thought that the Dipper's strong legs and feet were actually the key to its underwater foraging. This idea was fuelled by the common observation of how Dippers often enter the water without plunging in the manner of a Kingfisher, by simply wading in and not stopping, like a suicidal person trying to end it all.

Certainly, in shallow water Dippers probably can maintain position by clinging hard on to the stones of the riverbed, but in deeper water, it seems, they must resort to their flying technique. A powerful grip sometimes helps, but it appears never to be essential.

Whatever its methods, the Dipper is a completely adapted waterbird. Whenever you see one you are struck by its ease with the habitat. It will simply sit in shallow water like a fat businessman in a Jacuzzi; it will jump into water from rock or flight; it will wander over treacherous rapids with all the nonchalance of a cow moving to a different patch of grass. And, in the ultimate lifestyle statement for a bird of the rapids, it will even build its nest behind a waterfall.

Yet if you were to take the Dipper out of its habitat and put it on the woodland floor, among the leaf-litter, it wouldn't seem out of place at all. In fact, you could probably make it perch on a spade without too much difficulty. The Dipper may be an extreme bird, but it also stands out for its sheer ordinariness.

So perhaps you'd better check what your Robin is doing by the pond, after all.

Up periscope – a sight to excite the ire of an angler.

The Cormorant conundrum

A FEROCIOUS new debate is raging along our rivers, shattering the peace and quiet. This is a story mainly about people, and it has generated a great deal of press coverage and even a few prosecutions. It's all been caused by the recent arrival in our rivers of significant and increasing numbers of Cormorants. They come here mainly for the winter and, as is their custom, help themselves to a pound of fish a day, which they obtain by diving underwater. This predilection for scaly food has put them into direct competition with one of the most intransigent of inhabitants – the angler.

The problem is that Britain's river anglers once did not have to put up with any competition from Cormorants; the arrival of these birds is a recent event. Thirty years ago Cormorants were more or less confined to saltwater in Britain, and most of our birds still do breed on the coast and have little regard for leaving the sea. These days, though, perhaps through the influence of continental Cormorants, which breed in freshwater, Cormorants are now a common sight along many stretches of inland waterway. In fact, about 24,000 Cormorants winter in Britain every year, and about 10,000 of these do so on inland lakes or rivers.

Anglers don't welcome Cormorants on their patch and it is easy to understand why. If I were an angler, I would be more than a little miffed if a Cormorant came and disturbed my riverbank idyll, striking at the heart of my hobby. And if I was the owner of an inland fishery, I would be apoplectic at the thought of my living being under threat. I would also make a very simple, and – at face value – incontrovertible equation: Cormorants eat fish and therefore, especially where there are lots of them, they reduce the number and variety of fish available to me. Working on this logic, anglers are now up in arms about Cormorants. Feeling that their hobby is being spoilt by this so-called "Black Plague", they are demanding that action be taken to reduce Cormorant numbers.

But the situation is not quite as simple as it may seem. Rivers are complex ecosystems, and it is hard to prove that a single factor – namely predation by Cormorants – is causing a reduction in the amount of fish, certainly in the long term. Furthermore, in many waters there is little concrete proof that fish numbers are declining at all. Many anglers are highly reluctant to accept this, preferring what they see as the commonsense view – that the birds are destructive. And perhaps, in some locations, there's an element of truth in this. But most studies undertaken so far don't rule in the anglers' favour. In one investigation, for example, it was estimated that Cormorants take only about 10% of the fish in a given stretch of river, and these are mostly young fish of limited direct interest to anglers. It is highly likely that, in many areas, the anglers are simply wrong about the impact of Cormorants on their rivers. Other factors, including pollution, the weather, the patterns of fish movement and the nature of the riverbank, also come into play. Fish have other predators, and their numbers are also limited by disease and a host of other environmental factors. Any number of things, every day, can take their toll on the fish population. The important matter is how productive the river remains in the long term, to the benefit of the anglers and everybody else.

However, a good many anglers won't accept this, believing that the Cormorant conundrum has a simple solution, namely killing them. They blame the Cormorant not just for reducing fish numbers, but also more broadly for a perceived decline in the productivity of the river or lake habitat as a whole. Some even blame the Cormorant for causing the decline of Grey Herons, Kingfishers and Otters, which is a bit odd, since the populations of all these creatures are actually stable or increasing! If you try to be as open-minded as possible, you soon suspect that the dislike of Cormorants is itself a phenomenon worthy of attention.

One of the Cormorant's problems is that, being a large and obvious bird, it's an easy target for anger. You can easily catch one red-handed – i.e. with a flapping fish in its bill – whereas other threats to fish remain more hidden or nebulous. Cormorants are also far from charming. They are large, gawky birds, with a reptilian look and an unfortunate tendency to defecate in public. It would be impossible to imagine anglers dubbing the delightful Kingfishers the "Blue Plague", and most fishermen seem happy to share their river-bank with statuesque Grey Herons. But Cormorants excite neither respect nor admiration. Fishermen see them as greedy and wilfully destructive, injuring as many fish as they catch. Cormorants do everything but cherish fish, and that makes anglers very cross indeed.

But the sheer ill feeling directed towards Cormorants is alarming. Browse the web, and you'll find these black, web-footed birds described as vermin and compared to rats. There's even a website called "Cormorantbusters" – and that's one of the more considered ones! It is clear that a good many anglers would like all these birds shot out of the sky. While various arguments about control measures flow back and forth, it seems that, deep down, there is an anger towards Cormorants and their protectors that verges on hatred.

What, then, is at the heart of this problem?

I think that there are two issues here that don't always receive much attention. The first is that anglers tend to assume that the fish within their waters "belong" to them. Therefore, the Cormorants are arriving uninvited to eat "their" fish, stealing in like aquatic burglars. Now on inland closed fisheries, where the fish are introduced and are the property of the management, and where livelihoods are at stake, this is a reasonable position. But on rivers this right is highly questionable. The fish in rivers surely belong to us all, not just to anglers.

A second consideration in this debate is that the anglers might themselves feel misunderstood and threatened, and perhaps unrepresented by the wider public – and especially by conservationists. Some of their rhetoric smacks of paranoia and, on balance, I think they are perhaps not respected enough in their views. Many birdwatchers treat anglers with suspicion, and overlook the fact that fisherman love their waters and their fish with a rare and special passion, and can often be a force for good in the conservation of river ecosystems.

But passion is a powerful force, and sometimes it obscures the truth. For their part the fishermen need to accept that some of their arguments are groundless, and some need to calm down a bit or be reined in by their peers. Then, perhaps, peace on the riverbank can be restored.

Caring and sharing the Moorhen way

The nest of a Moorhen is a bulky structure of vegetation.

THERE CAN be few more idyllic scenes than a pair of Moorhens dutifully feeding their chicks in the gentle sheltered shallows of a river. The youngsters are exceptionally appealing, with their tiny black, fluffy bodies, reddish heads and absurd little stumps for wings; they beg for food by bleating pathetically, and it's hard not to feel your heart melting as you find yourself rooting for their survival. The parents, meanwhile, carry out their never-ending feeding duties stoically, always patient with their young, always managing to appear well turned out, with their silky-smooth coal black plumage and neat white flashes on the flanks and tail. And their laboured swimming action, nodding their heads with every stroke of their feet – like a cyclist battling uphill – only serves to make their work look that much tougher. Yet they never seem to shirk their tasks. It's all wholesome family life: admirable, noble and uplifting.

And what do we find when we look beneath this veneer of respectability? Even more admirable respectability! It turns out that some Moorhen pairs are able to enlist help from unattached adults in feeding their young, making their parenting something of a community project. It is not clear whether these helpers benefit in the short term, but they don't have sexual relations with either male or female. They are simply helping, no more and no less.

Co-operation in Moorhens is something of a theme, and it starts early in life. The Moorhen is one of very few British birds that uses willing child labour during the breeding period. A pair frequently attempts two, and sometimes three broods in the course of a single season, and when this happens the young from the earliest brood often help their parents in caring for subsequent broods. These youngsters have not yet left home, so while they are still hanging around it seems crazy not to put them to some useful task. The teenagers will assist with nest refurbishment, bring snacks for the young, brood the newly hatched chicks under their bellies and, remarkably, will even do stints of incubation – that most critical of all nesting duties. It seems that young Moorhens are thrown into a world of responsibility almost from the start, and their efforts are of genuine help to the nesting pair.

As female Moorhens grow up, an even more surprising, and exceptionally unusual type of co-operation will sometimes happen. On occasion, it seems that a mother and one of her daughters from a previous year actually make a joint nesting attempt. They build a nest together, they both lay their eggs in the same nest, and they co-operate in feeding the resulting young. What a great role model for feminism: an older female empowering a younger one in the important task of raising kids! It's hard not to be enthusiastic about this kind of mentoring, and wonder why a good many other birds don't do exactly the same.

It's only when you look a little more closely at this last type of arrangement that the whole thing takes on a slightly more sinister – or at least less radiantly healthy – aspect. Where, you might ask, is the father in all of this? Somebody has to provide the sperm and, as we know, Moorhen males are not the absentee type; they make good, hard-working fathers. He has to be on the scene somewhere. And so he is, ever-present. And that is when you realise that mother and daughter are actually sharing his charms. Male Moorhens are extremely fierce in defending their territories, and it is not in their nature to allow any egg-producing female to wander off-site and be impregnated by another bird. No, both mother and daughter have to use the same male for sperm. It's his territory and, as incumbent, he will do his best to make sure that all the eggs are his.

So now, if you know another thing about Moorhen relationships, you might

begin to feel a little queasy. Although the pair-bond between adult male and female usually lasts just a single season, it is by no means uncommon for the same pairing to be taken up year on year, especially if the habitat is a stable one. Thus it some-times happens that a young Moorhen pairing co-operatively with her mother will be sharing the sperm of the bird that is actually her father. That's not a very pleasant thought and, indeed, the results are not very pleasant either: inbred chicks have a very low rate of survival. It is, perhaps, stretching the spirit of family co-operation a little far for our tastes; it certainly never happened in The Waltons.

A young Moorhen (foreground) helps its parent feed newly hatched chicks.

Some moorhen specialists see a sensible strategy lying behind this behaviour. It is always difficult for young birds of any species to make their initial breeding attempt – they simply don't have the experience or skills. That is why, think these specialists, the adult female Moorhen gives her daughter a helping hand first time round. Somehow, though, the idea of enlisting the father's help as well cannot surely be part of the plan.

There is one more type of Moorhen co-operation that is also a little suspect, too. This is the very common practice of laying your eggs in the nest of another bird – usually another Moorhen, though very occasionally something else. Known also as intraspecific brood parasitism, this is a way of maximising your production without the effort of raising the subsequent chicks yourself.

Don't be fooled into thinking that it's voluntary, though. Moorhens parasitise their neighbours furtively, stealing into the nest and laying the extra egg while the owner isn't looking. Adoption is costly for an adult, and it would not be pleased if it found out that one of the pleading bills in its nest did not belong to a chick from its own genetic stock. Moorhens, to their core, are mighty co-operative birds; but there are limits!

SCRUB

Underrated undergrowth

SCRUB IS underappreciated. No birdwatcher ever sets off saying 'Let's visit some scrub,' as they might if they were heading for an estuary or a marsh. Even the word "scrub" has a ring of the underclass about it. Yet this unruly and unsung mixture of bushes and undergrowth is one of Britain's most important bird habitats. We might not give it much of a thought, but birds most certainly do.

ONE OF the problems for scrub's publicists is that their client is quite difficult to define. Essentially, it is land covered with thickets and bushes, rather than trees, with more or less open patches in between, where flowers and grasses grow. Scrub forms a halfway house between open country and woodland; if you wanted to be rude you could call it degraded grassland or incomplete tree cover. And it is usually transitory, tending to occupy ground where woodland has been cleared and the land left abandoned, leaving bushes to fill the vacuum. But, if the plot remains unmanaged, the seeds of large trees invariably germinate amongst the fallow patches of scrub, and over the course of time they are able to grow tall, cast a canopy and become, in effect, a woodland once again. During this inexorable process of succession, scrub occupies the land like some kind of squatter, to be evicted when the rightful owner returns. There are places, though, where scrub persists for many years without ever giving way to woodland. This often happens when the land is heavily grazed: the animals cannot penetrate into well-established bushes, but they do mow up any over-ambitious tree shoots, and thus help maintain the scrubby *status quo*. In other places, mainly on nature reserves, conservation volunteers – another species of pruning animal – can be commandeered into doing the same job, fuelled by tea and biscuits instead of fresh grazing. And in scattered sites, controlled burning can also keep woodland at bay.

So, despite its lowly status, there is a lot of

scrub around in Britain today, both of the transitory, woodland-edge sort and of the more permanent, managed sort. And the birds love it in all its forms, because it provides valuable resources that are harder to find elsewhere. These are, most importantly, a thick tangle of cover for concealment and shelter; and an open shrub layer canopy that, in season, is groaning with edible plant and insect life.

The scrubby dormitory

If you visit a patch of scrub in the midst of winter, you might not be particularly impressed with its birdlife. There may be little visible activity or noise. But the silence you hear is only the silence of waiting, because one of the great benefits of winter scrub is that it can act as a dormitory for hosts of birds.

We often do not recognise that every resident bird has three, not two fundamental needs in winter. In our gardens we provide lots of food, and if we are diligent, water. But shelter is often lacking. We adore our winter birds by day, but they disappear from our radar as they retreat into the darkness at night, and we forget that they must find a secure and sheltered roost site if they are to return tomorrow. But a nearby patch of vacant ground with low, thick bushes can act as a communal shelter for some of our garden birds. Evergreen shrubs in particular, such as holly, or even the much reviled Leylandii cypress, provide ideal conditions for overnight survival. The mature trees of woodland are too open and tall, and the undergrowth of woods is often not dense enough. What birds need on cold nights are deep thickets.

Many of the birds that sleep inside scrubby growth do so in groups. Blackbirds, because of their noisy bickering before settling down, are among the most obvious, going to sleep with the peace and decorum of a party of schoolchildren on their first night of a trip away from home. Their noisy "*chink, chink*" notes carry across the neighbourhood, and the brouhaha is hard to miss. Blackbirds, you see, are not naturally very sociable birds, generally tense in each other's company; yet the shared need for a safe roost site brings them to the same place, and they simply have to get on with each other. Prior to sleeping, they sort out who perches where with a little aggression and a lot of raised voices. In fact some scientists suspect that all this fuss and clamour helps them to release excess energy before darkness falls.

If you visit the right patch of scrub at the end of a winter afternoon, you can witness the arrival of a somewhat less vociferous group of birds, the finches. On a cold night small bodies will stream in throughout the last hour of light, arriving in parties that coalesce into large groups before retiring into the scrub. By nightfall, several hundred individual birds may crowd the branches of the most sheltered spots, making calls of low volume but high intensity. Enticingly for the birdwatcher, roosts often hold a wide range of different species, including more unusual ones such as Bramblings and Siskins, as well as the Greenfinches and Chaffinches that make up the bulk of the membership. Some of these birds may have come from as much as ten kilometres away, just for the privilege of roosting in this favoured site.

Where large patches of scrub form in an otherwise open area, they may attract the impressive communal roosts of Starlings. While single Starlings look a bit scruffy, and in small groups they resemble gangs of unkempt kids misspending their youth, Starlings in large numbers around their roosts can form a quite awesome spectacle. Having spent the day spread out over the countryside, they – like the finches – converge on the roost-site as darkness approaches and gather in flocks that increase in size by the minute. But unlike the finch flocks, which usually level out in the tens or hundreds of birds, the Starlings keep gathering until they become swarms, covering entire trees and bushes in closely-packed, animated dots, like feathered leaves.

As the Starlings fly in to their pre-roost assembly in nearby trees or wires, they make little noise except for the swoosh of their wings overhead. But as soon as they land they become involved in animated discourses with their neighbours. With hundreds of conversations going on, the volume rises until, despite it being known colloquially as a "murmuration", the sound becomes more like a sustained screech. Finally, just before it is time to sink down into the scrub for the night, the whole flock may take off and perform some aerial manoeuvres, for reasons that still puzzle scientists. The mass of birds twists and turns as if were a single organism moving across the sky, with waves of birds crashing on imaginary beaches and billowing from side to side, yet always being reined in to the flock, as though on elastic. This extraordinary demonstration of numbers soon subsides, and the birds at last settle down into the scrub, where they will spend a restless night.

Starlings collect together in their pre-roost assembly.

A season of plenty

The communal roosts of birds begin to dwindle almost as soon as the calendar year starts, and by the beginning of March they are a shadow of their midwinter selves. Now, though, the scrub acquires a new set of occupants, birds that are drawn less to the protective structure of the habitat and more towards the feeding opportunities it provides. Blackthorn shrubs lead the way in this revolution, throwing out their soft white blooms in the early days of spring, attracting insects from hiding and drawing birds towards this welcome extra protein. They are joined by hazel and willow catkins, and finally by the leaves, with each layer of vegetation sheltering more and more insect life. At this time of the year the woods may still be starkly leafless, but the scrub is already humming with customers.

And this early richness is just the start. Late spring ushers in the flowering roses, and the herb layer around the bushes thickens into a jumble of stems, thorns and flowers. With all this growth exposed to the sunlight, the insect life proliferates and, lured by the irresistible combination of foliage in which to hide and insects on which to feed, the birds arrive to take up territory and breed.

Many of these new inhabitants are migratory insect-eating birds that belong to the same family: the warblers. These are the sort of creatures that madden birdwatchers, being both inveterate skulkers and incapable of staying still. They zip around bushes, gleaning insects from the leaves, occasionally popping their heads out to check for danger but never coming right out into the open – except for the odd aerial sally after a particularly tempting flying invertebrate. Identifying these birds is a fine art, based upon glimpses and impressions. And that's just how warbler fanatics like it: too good a view

The effervescent Whitethroat often sings in flight.

demystifies the quarry, and reduces its appeal.

Many summer visitors to the scrub have loud and memorable songs; this is partly because they need to be heard amidst the tangled vegetation, which is hardly the ideal site for parading your plumage. The most celebrated is the Nightingale, of course, but there are many others here, each with its own style and pitch. The Garden Warbler speaks in a babble, the Willow Warbler sighs a soft descending scale, the Whitethroat blurts out an abrupt burst of scratchy notes, and the Grasshopper Warbler just reels off a double-note at twenty-four to the second, sounding just like a freewheeling bicycle.

Hasty does it

Some of these scrub-dwellers, here only for the summer bonanza, follow rushed schedules and make only brief attachments. The Whitethroat, for instance, a high-voltage dynamo that often bursts into the air when singing and hangs there for a short while like a puppet dangling on a string, is a capricious species, forever changing the borders of its territory and forming passing relationships. Males sometimes keep two females at once, and some have more than one territory – although the situation can change from day to day. Relationships rarely last beyond the first brood. These birds build nests, but then break them down as they build again. Long before people ever did, the Whitethroat lives in a throwaway society.

The Garden Warbler arrives quite late and is not usually present before May. In common with most small insectivorous birds, though, it tries to pack the raising of two broods into its short summer season. Things are relatively straightforward for the first set of chicks, but the

second set is racing against the clock from the moment the eggs are fertilised.

Garden Warblers, you see, begin migration in August and by September need to have cleared the country. This leaves a very small window for the hapless chicks to make their way in the world, but somehow they manage. Remarkably, as little as four weeks may pass between the moment these youngsters chip their way out of the egg and the first few wing-beats of their great journey.

Fuelling up

These plucky voyagers do, however, get a head start from their habitat. For it is in the autumn, more than any other time, that scrub really comes into its own. This is the season when just about every bird, whether its normal home is woods, fields or marshes, makes its way, hungrily, to thicket country.

The reason for this is simple: berries. If you take a roll call of all the usual scrub plants – brambles, holly, elder, hawthorn, blackthorn and spindle, for example – you will find that a high proportion of them produce berries. Indeed, scrub has more berries available than any other habitat. There are red ones and black ones, even a few pink and white ones, and a variety of different sizes to suit different gapes. Berries are easy to find, easy to deal with and provide lots of healthy nutriment. They are autumn's prime commodity, the answer to every bird's needs. Residents eat them, and migrants – desperate to fatten up in time for their journeys – devour them. For a few short weeks the daily stress of finding food is replaced by an easy binge for all.

No wonder that birds flock to scrub. In autumn, the thickets are often filled with parties of youngsters gathered together for security. They spend their days moving from bush to bush, one after the other, to find fruit and insects. The berry-laden branches sometimes become battlegrounds, as birds fight to protect their personal berry supplies. This often seems to be a waste of energy, with arguments being as much over personal space as anything else. Everywhere, though, in whatever way they can, birds are guzzling berries.

Although it may seem as though the birds are ransacking the bushes, this feeding frenzy suits the plants, too. Most berry eaters are only in it for the fleshy pulp of the fruit; harder seeds pass through the gut and are summarily excreted. A few of these seeds fall on suitable ground and

Haw berries are much appreciated by Redwings.

germinate, completing the plant's dispersal process. This is why berries are so easy to find and process; the plants, you might say, "want" their fruit to be consumed. Their colours are designed to lure birds: red ones are obvious even to us, while bluer ones give off ultraviolet reflectance, which most birds can probably detect. And they are meant to taste good, to make them easier to ingest.

In woodland, the early autumn foliage is thick and the trees are tall, making the berries harder to get at, especially in the wind. But in scrub, with its low cover, berries are more naturally accessible to their dispersers. The berry-laden bushes work like "special offer" displays in supermarkets: you cannot resist them, and you shouldn't.

Rest for the weary

Berries on bushes are not just beneficial for resident birds and for migrants preparing to depart, they are also a welcome resource for the countless thousands of continental birds that come here as winter visitors. Such birds often tuck into our stocks of fruit the moment they make landfall. And indeed, several species that come here from the continent for the cold season, such as Redwings and Fieldfares, spend most of their first month or two moving nomadically around Britain in a quest for suitable patches of berry-laden scrub.

Some of our winter visitors touch down in desperate need. Migration can be perilous at times, and sometimes birds have to battle wind and weather for many hours before they struggle over the finish line. When they stop, as they often do, on inhospitable parts of our coast and in the teeth of a howling gale, berries are probably the last thing on their mind. All they want is some thick bushes offering a stable perch and a bit of shelter.

And that's another great thing about scrub: it might be a low-grade transition habitat in much of Britain, but in some cold, rain-lashed, windswept areas it is the consummate peak of vegetation. In such places scrub is natural and scrub is king. And for our weary arriving migrants, it is also their lifeline.

The skulking Nightingale lives in deep shade.

The real Nightingale

THERE ARE two types of Nightingales in Britain: real ones and fake ones. The fake ones are by far the more numerous. Fake Nightingales are heard in gardens throughout Britain at night, and turn up almost anywhere that a beautiful bird song overwhelms somebody's emotions. Real Nightingales are actually pretty rare, and are confined to the edge of woodland and thick scrub.

The fact that there are fake Nightingales at all speaks volumes for the real thing. The best human singers make waves too; worldwide there are thousands of Elvis Presley impersonators, some of them actually making a living doing nothing else. This suggests that, whatever your tastes, the original must have been pretty special. Wherever there has been good music, there have been its imitators clinging to the coattails of stardom.

So what is it about the real Nightingale, the one with perfect credentials, to have spawned such a following? What was it that lit the literary tinder of Keats? How can such a peripheral member of Britain's bird fauna – it is a scarce species and only here between April and August – have managed to make such an impression?

Well, there's no doubt that it sings well – superbly well. It is perhaps unique among British songbirds in its range of pitch and, in particular, volume. Hearing one close up, it is remarkable how the bird can whisper to you one moment and shout at you the next, all in the course of a single exultant phrase. The impact takes you aback, and beguiles you; the performer seems to have a sense of the dramatic. Furthermore a Nightingale seems deliberately to hold you in suspense between phrases, so that you are never sure what might come next, or whether you have reached the limit of the bird's rich repertoire.

All famous singers have their trademark hit song – the three-minute wonder that immortalises a career. And the Nightingale is no exception. It's not a song as such, but part of a song. About a quarter of its phrases begin with a series of slow, pure, sad notes that build up to a crescendo before exploding into a loud but perfunctory trill. This type of phrase is pure Nightingale, with its mixture of melancholy and brio; it is hard to hear it without smiling to yourself at the bird's audacity. Like that proverbial hit record, you can listen again and again without the wonder ever quite fading.

But the physical properties of the Nightingale's song, however impressive, cannot explain its allure. There are other birds that have comparable songs, and even more tuneful ones, but the general public hears little about them. There must be something else about the Nightingale that makes it stand out, some kind of star quality.

It is sometimes said in the entertainment industry, only partly facetiously, that death is the best career move an artist can make. Jimi Hendrix, Kurt Cobain and Eva Cassidy are all the more celebrated now because their careers were cut cruelly short. There is something about an artist lost that makes us want to preserve them as they were, keeping what we have. Perhaps the same sort of emotion takes over when we hear the Nightingale. For it is something we hear only occasionally in our lives. The bird only sings here between late April and early June; its career is a brief one, and we hear it in its prime only at the height of spring.

There is also a mystery about this bird, because we hardly ever set eyes upon it – like those reclusive pop stars whose retiring nature only adds to their mystique. Even if we hear the Nightingale every spring, day after day and night after night, we never regularly see it. Nightingales are unusual among songbirds for keeping out of sight while singing. They live in thick scrub and feed on the ground deep in the shadows. And when – after much effort – you finally do spot one, the sight is invariably a disappointment. It is merely a small brownish bird, with not a pattern or marking to distinguish it. So Nightingales do well to hide away, leaving their essential character to the imagination of their listeners.

But what really makes the Nightingale special is, of course, its celebrated habit of singing at night. On the whole, very few birds do this and those that do are not much to listen to – birds like Grasshopper Warblers, which sound like freewheeling bicycles and Black Redstarts, whose song recalls the sound of paper being crumpled up! So, when the sun goes down, the Nightingale has little competition. As darkness falls, the last Blackbirds and Song Thrushes gradually peter out and the Nightingale is left to dominate the airwaves.

Contrary to popular perception, the Nightingale sings regularly by day, too. But the very fact that people don't realise this simply shows how the Nightingale loses its impact against the everyday bird chorus. If the Nightingale didn't sing at night, would we take very much notice of it? Probably not. So it seems, then, that setting is the key. The Nightingale has secured the most exclusive slot in which to weave its way into people's consciousness. It is a lone voice, concealed by darkness, singing with power and abandon on the most romantic nights of the year. No wonder the poets are moved to celebrate it, and to muse of life, love and loss.

And those tribute singers, the ones we hear in the gardens? Those are merely Robins. They are close relatives of the Nightingale, but not the real thing. They sing incessantly through the year, demystifying themselves by sitting on spades and living close to people. Their song is not bad, not bad at all – but it's all in the setting, you see.

Nightingales sing by day as well as by night.

Speed-dating in Willow Warblers

UNTIL RECENTLY it has been very hard for scientists to unravel what makes individuals of any species attractive to one another. This difficult area of research is rendered all the trickier by our confused ideas about the nature of human love and relationships. But several studies of small birds have recently shown that some species can be very cold and calculating when it comes to this area of their lives. Literally calculating, in fact.

The Willow Warbler is a small insectivorous bird that abounds in scrubby vegetation throughout Britain. It is particularly drawn to young birches and, of course, willows, where its olive-green coloration enables it to disappear from view among the leaves. About the size of a Blue Tit, the Willow Warbler is a summer visitor to Britain, with the first birds making landfall towards the end of March. Once here, the males sing a deliciously gentle song, easily blown away on the breeze. Their phrase is a short downward scale, slightly hesitant at first but then sliding down more sweetly until, at the bottom, it peters out to a somewhat inchoate conclusion.

The males arrive about ten days before the females, and use their songs to defend a territory that will provide all the resources the owner needs for the summer – food, shelter and a nest-site. Not surprisingly, competition over territories is fierce, and song-duels and physical fights between males are quite common around this time. Soon, however, the birds sort themselves out and maintain an uneasy truce around their border areas. By the time the females arrive, some sort of order has been established.

The Willow Warbler is a short-lived, high-octane bird. Having spent a month or two migrating here, it is already constrained by time

The female Willow Warbler monitors the song rate of its suitor.

as soon as begins breeding. The females – for they are the "choosing sex", as is typical with birds – must find a mate without delay. If they dither, they may sacrifice their chance of bringing up two batches of young instead of just one, which is a serious loss of potential productivity. So they have to move fast in choosing a worthy mate who will provide good genetic material. But where to start? The answer is, effectively, speed-dating. Once the females settle upon the neighbourhood where they intend to breed (usually close to where they were born), they will make their choice by embarking on a tour of the nearby territories and territory-holding males. It is not known exactly how many suitors they will visit, but the number is probably in double figures for most individuals. Within each territory they remain only for about 10–20 minutes before moving on to the next, and while there they monitor the rate of singing of the male present. These choosy females don't exactly carry clipboards as they go, but they are definitely taking measurements and awarding marks.

It seems that the females are seeking males with the highest song output, for it is these – scientists have found – that pair up most rapidly with the newly arrived talent. The sheer regularity of a male's singing is comparatively easy for a female to measure, and is the critical factor behind her selection.

But what does song output actually show? The theory goes that the frequency of a male's singing is directly linked to the quality of his territory. When a male is advertising for a mate he has nothing on his mind except food and sex. He can sing all day if required, but he must fuel his efforts with frequent feeding bouts throughout this time, otherwise he will simply run out of steam.

It follows that, the easier the food is to obtain, the more frequently the male can sing. If he is in a good territory, he needs to make only short trips into the foliage to satisfy his needs quickly and can then return refreshed. In poor territory, however, he will need to interrupt his singing bouts more often and for longer as he searches a wider area for fuel. It seems that, just by monitoring a male's singing for a short time, the female can appreciate these differences, and can make an informed choice as a result.

It doesn't say much for the affection between two birds when one is choosing the other only for the quality of his territory. We humans may be appalled at this, but don't we make exactly these choices from time to time, however much we may couch it in the rhetoric of romance? When a young, worldly woman marries an elderly millionaire, she is usually doing little

more than metaphorically recording his singing output.

And the female Willow Warblers at least have an excuse for their strategy. They will shortly have mouths to feed, and male Willow Warblers are notorious slouches and womanisers. The chances are that the female will take on the lion's share of feeding the chicks, for there is very little in the way of a relationship between the sexes, and minimal partnership in parenting. No, the female must be judicious in what she is buying into. She may not have much confidence in her partner, but the quality of his territory is a good tangible asset, and one that will not usually change throughout the short breeding season. As a convenient by-product, the males with better territories will probably also provide superior genes.

Let's face it, if you had no love to lose and plenty of booty to gain, you'd probably make the same choice yourself. And pretty quickly, too.

The assiduous female Willow Warbler listens very carefully to the songs of all the males it meets.

The Fieldfare's secret weapon

Fieldfares bombard intruders at the nest and pelt them with faeces.

WHEN IT visits us in the winter to enjoy our mild, damp climate and well-stocked scrub and hedgerows, the Fieldfare is an easy bird to overlook. It disperses over our countryside and mucks in with its close and more familiar relatives, such as Blackbirds and Song Thrushes. Like them it combs fields and lawns for worms in the soil, and guzzles berries from trees and shrubs. In the winter it behaves in an unexceptional manner, although it tends to be a little on the irritable side.

In short, you probably wouldn't imagine the Fieldfare capable of anything particularly out of the ordinary. It doesn't have any unusual plumage features or physiological quirks. There is nothing in its feeding behaviour that differs from that of the other thrushes. Its profile remains so low that you could have a lifelong interest in nature and never realise that the Fieldfare existed at all.

But the Fieldfare does, in fact, do something exceptionally unusual; a feat performed by no other thrushes (so far as is known) and, indeed, no other British bird at all. Something in its genetic makeup has sent the Fieldfare out on an extraordinary limb, providing one of Europe's most remarkable bird stories.

The setting is the mixed wooded country of north-central Europe and Scandinavia. Here the Fieldfare ranks among the most abundant of all birds, inhabiting the ubiquitous tapestry of interspersed field and copse typical of this part of the world. In the spring the Fieldfare is sociable, usually nesting in rather loose colonies. Indeed, these colonies are often spread over such a wide area that they may more accurately be described as suburbs. In places many hundreds of nests may be placed close enough for some to be in sight of one another, and the adults manage – with typical Scandinavian tolerance – to work the same

feeding sites without coming to blows. Thus a Fieldfare suburb is a place where community is important and resources are shared. Indeed, other birds often share these suburbs, too. Bramblings and Redwings, for example, often select these sites over those where the big thrushes are absent. Property prices – metaphorically speaking – must be high hereabouts.

Into this Fieldfare Shangri-La come intermittent threats of danger. This is hardly surprising: any such close-packed gathering of prey is irresistible to predators. Indeed, you might well wonder why the birds should gather in such close proximity at all, given the risk of attracting such unwelcome attention. And when an unsuspecting predator wanders into the neighbourhood, its eyes must pop wide open at the sight of all those birds, eggs and chicks stacked together like cakes on a baker's counter. Perhaps it wonders why it alone has stumbled upon this bounty. But any misgivings soon give way to temptation, and that – it soon turns out – is a fatal mistake.

At first the peril is all the Fieldfares'. The sight of a marauding Crow, for example, is the trigger for extreme alarm. An attack could mean the loss of young and perhaps the waste of a whole breeding season. In one brief moment, all the Fieldfares in the district are on red alert.

Nobody quite knows what the trigger is for action, but first one, then two and soon many Fieldfares launch themselves into the air. And instead of the usual response to a predator, which is to fly off in the hope of distracting it, the Fieldfares remain on station, close to their nest sites. All of them begin to call loudly, offering up discordant and unpleasant rattling noises that, to any sensible intruder, would be a good cue to depart. And with lots of birds airborne and at their noisiest, the rumpus simply attracts more and more angry, unsettled Fieldfares.

Predators are used to this kind of thing. They attract disturbance wherever they go, being regularly mobbed, scolded and even attacked in the line of duty. They would not expect a warm welcome anywhere. But the fieldfare assault they are about to experience is different; it goes beyond nuisance. Once the offending Crow fails to take the hint, it has had its final warning. An extraordinary form of predator deterrence is unleashed.

It is quite a simple strategy, really. A Fieldfare flies up, stalls and then swoops down towards the intruder. As it gets close it lets off a peculiar squealing sound and then, aiming carefully, delivers a gooey bomb of faeces straight on to the Crow's carefully preened plumage. Before the Crow has time to compose itself, a second Fieldfare dives down and does the same, ejecting its package seconds after the first. The next follows moments later and, within seconds, the predator becomes a great deal less threatening as it find itself pelted by a hailstorm of Fieldfare excreta.

Such attacks can last several minutes. The thrushes are clearly armed enough to keep going until their bombing runs have had the desired effect. Most predators retreat very rapidly under this onslaught. As far as is known, they do not return.

Now it is easy to make light of this unusual bombardment; it is extraordinary, almost amusing. But in reality it can be dangerous to the victim. Uric acid is not a pleasant substance, and it can have the effect of compromising the waterproofing on a bird's feathers and thus consigning its owner to a slow death. Although such outcomes are undoubtedly rare, the threat is sufficient to make the borders of the Fieldfare colony almost uniquely safe against similar intrusions.

There are many other birds that use partly digested food as a deterrent to predators. Some, such as Fulmars, eject foul-smelling effluvia from their front end rather than their rear, while others also eject faeces. But what is remarkable about the Fieldfare's nest defence is the apparent co-ordination of the attack and the degree to which it is sustained. Such behaviour has not been documented in any other European species.

Amazingly, the predator bombing only takes place for a small part of the Fieldfare's breeding season, when well-incubated eggs or chicks are in the nests. Before and after there is no such display. And, of course, when the birds arrive in Britain the memory of their antics fades away and they can melt into our countryside without us having any suspicion of what a Fieldfare, suitably enraged, is capable of.

The Fieldfare as we in Britain know it, a harmless consumer of berries and discarded fruit.

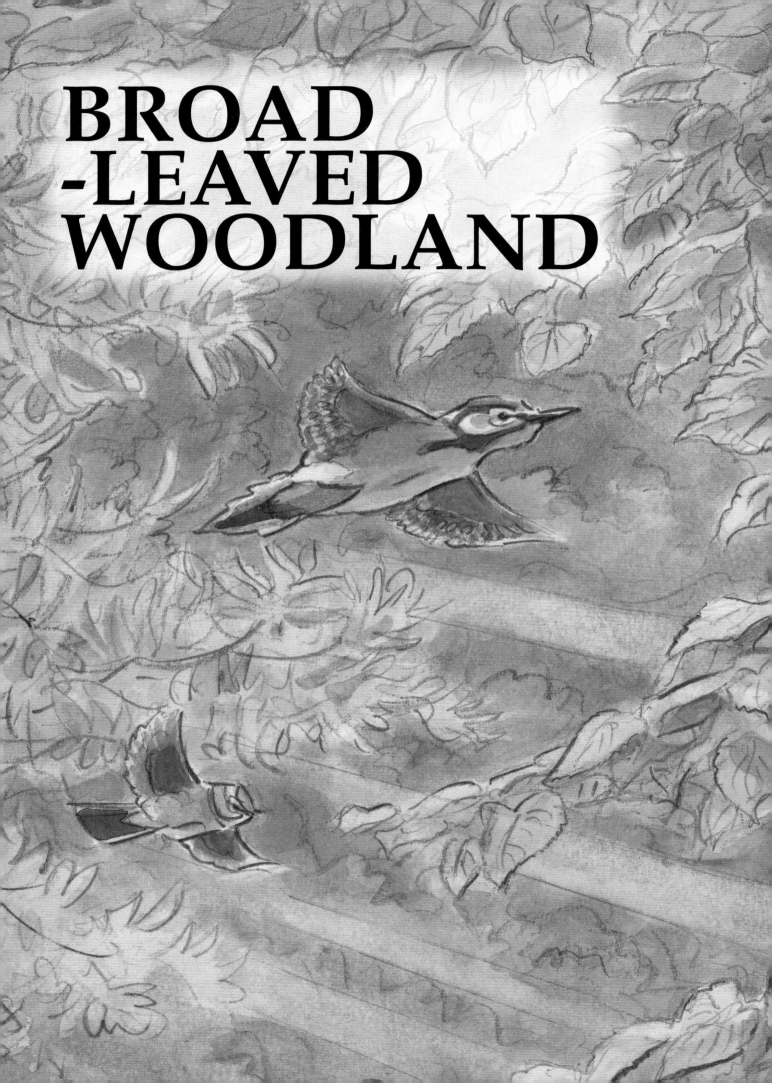

BROAD -LEAVED WOODLAND

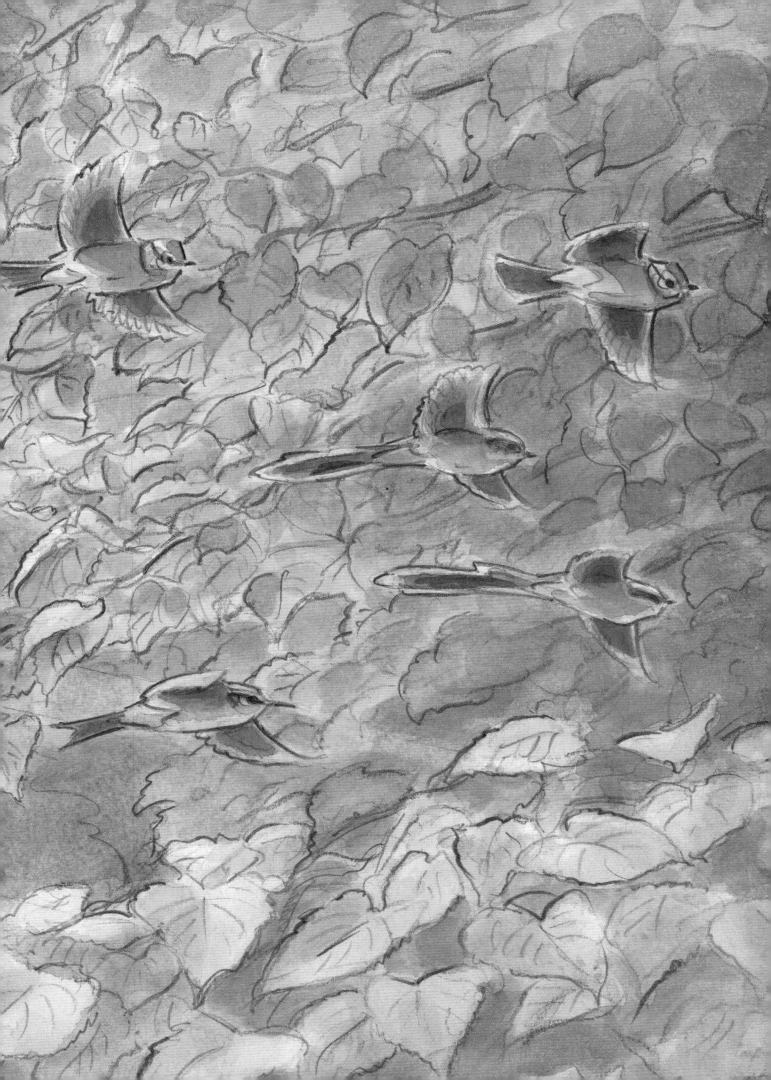

The green curtain

THE WOODLAND always teases. If you visit in the depths of winter, birds seem to be absent and the stark branches are depressingly lifeless. Yet the birds are here alright, they are just hidden away. The same is often true at the height of summer, when all the activity of this wondrously rich habitat is concealed behind a green curtain of leaves.

IT IS very easy to visit a deciduous woodland in winter and be disappointed with the show of birds – or rather the lack of it. In fact, you might take a few hours' walk in December or January and see nothing of consequence at all. But there are good reasons for this. Now that autumn has faded away, food is much less concentrated than it was during September and October, and the birds are following fewer clues to fewer feeding sites. Furthermore, even those that are here can be very quiet in these lean months, often feeding quietly on the woodland floor with all the quiet reverence of archaeologists at a dig.

But if you do come across birds in a winter woodland, it will often be plenty of them all at once. You might be momentarily overwhelmed, suddenly realising that the wood is alive after all. That is because most of the smaller inhabitants prefer, at this season, to travel around in flocks. So you will rarely come across species such as tits, Treecreepers and Goldcrests in isolation, but instead as part of a "wave" of birds, moving in a relentless but seemingly random pattern through the trees.

Most of these birds have gathered together primarily for protection. The combined vigilance of many pairs of eyes ensures that most approaching predators, such as Sparrowhawks, are quickly spotted, allowing everyone to scatter and thus to disrupt the hunter's concentration. This scattering is aided by a common language, a series of sounds that are cross-cultural and recognised by all. Different bird species rarely take notice of one another's vocalisations, but alarm calls are understood by the whole small bird community.

Security is not the only advantage of flocking. Birds in a flock naturally spend most of the day feeding, and this allows the most resourceful ones to take advantage of working in a crowd. They may do this indirectly, by observing other species foraging and learning new techniques for locating food or dealing with it; or they may be more direct and uncharitably rob their companions of what they have found. This food theft, which is known more grandly as kleptoparasitism, is no minority sport, either. Birds frequently hijack smaller or subordinate individuals, both of their own species and of others, for ill-gotten gain. Coal and Marsh Tits, for example, are forever being mugged by their more pugnacious relatives, Blue and Great Tits. In the victims' cases it must only be the heightened security offered by a flock that keeps them there at all.

Marsh Tits don't make their own flocks, but will join flocks of other birds passing through their territory.

Some species are inveterate flock members and keep company with others throughout the day, moving along with the wave. Tits, especially, often form the core of the informal flock and may be termed "carrier species"; without them there would be no impetus for gathering together. Long-tailed Tits are highly unusual in that they form permanent groups of family members that roost together in a huddle at night to keep each other warm. Upon awakening they are a ready-made flock, to which individuals of other species are soon attracted.

But the informality of the flock, which changes in composition through the day and through the season, also gives a chance for less sociable species of the wood to become temporary

Reflecting the many niches of woodland – the Treecreeper creeps up, the Nuthatch runs down.

members. Birds such as Lesser Spotted Woodpeckers, Marsh Tits and Nuthatches generally live like stockbrokers, keeping themselves to themselves within the territorial borders of their own clearly defined patch. But when a roaming flock passes through their territory, they readily join the gathering, finding it strangely compelling. As soon as the flock moves beyond their boundaries, they split off and become solitary again, just like a country squire joining ramblers for a brief stroll around his own grounds before retiring to his manor house.

Each to a niche

In many ways, these woodland winter flocks are not so different from the gatherings of waders you see on mudflats, in that all species are working the same general area, but differ in the niches that they occupy and the way in which they exploit them. Watch carefully, and you will see that, even while the flock remains cohesive, some birds stay in the trees, while others visit the ground or remain just above it; and some scour the branches or trunks, while others check out the twigs or

prefer the dead wood. These are living examples of birds going their separate ecological ways. To take a simplified example, Great Tits often feed on the ground, working the leaf-litter, whereas Long-tailed Tits don't. Long-tailed Tits are tiny, and probably not strong enough to flick dead leaves aside as the Great Tit can; and their long tails, designed as a counterbalance for their foliage acrobatics, would be an encumbrance on the ground. But the mesh of thin twigs utilised by Long-tailed Tits doesn't suit the Great Tit, as this is a proportionally heavier species with larger feet, and the twigs would get in its way. Neither would the Great Tit be able to subsist on miniscule moth eggs and scale insects, as the Long-tailed Tit can. There are many such distinctions as these.

One of the more singular lifestyles in a woodland bird community, and one easily appreciated by even the most novice observer, is that of the Treecreeper. This is a small, mouse-like bird with a pleasing pure-white breast and mottled brown back, that spends its days climbing up the trunks and larger branches of trees, adhering so closely to the bark that it seems to be in some way attached to it. The Treecreeper never wavers from its rhythmic feeding method, which involves climbing up a trunk or side-branch, flying down to the bottom of the next and climbing up again, and it rarely hunts anywhere but tree surfaces (although confused treecreepers have been known to scale trouser legs or even bicycles by mistake). The Treecreeper is an insectivore, and the cracks and fissures of tree bark are such a reliable source of insect life that it never needs – if you'll pardon the pun – to branch out. The bark of trees is said to be one of the most stable habitats around, so few birds fit more snugly into their niche than a Treecreeper.

The Treecreeper shares its habitat with another climbing species, the Nuthatch. Yet the two differ in all sorts of ways, both subtle and obvious, that combine to demonstrate how well woodland serves all its different customers. In contrast to the Treecreeper, which has a thin, slightly curved bill, the Nuthatch has a straight, sharp brute of a beak, perfectly designed to beat the living daylights out of hard nuts such as beech mast and acorns. It lodges them in the bark (the same bark from which the Treecreeper vacuums up insects) and hacks them open, using the weight of its whole body to do so. Nuthatches usually survive winter by storing autumn nuts away in these fissures and retrieving them when required. But in summer they gladly glean insects from the cracks as the Treecreeper does.

Nuthatches can perform a trick that Treecreepers cannot – and neither can any other

bird in the world, come to that: they can climb down trees head-first. They do this by getting a good grip on the bark with one foot and momentarily using this as support for the whole body, while the free foot works its way to the next grip, and so on. It sounds laborious but works perfectly well in practice, although the bird's progress is a little jerky. Overall it means that Nuthatches can explore all the major limbs of a tree in any direction, and can gain a competitive advantage over other species by looking down a tree while everyone else is working upwards.

Both of these tree-hugging birds typically confine their work to the nooks and crannies of the surface, without exploiting the rich feeding sites beneath the bark. This sort of hard labour is left to those who have the tools – namely, the woodpeckers. Woodpeckers have fearsome bills and reinforced skulls that are designed for the bruising business of excavation. They exploit this adaptation to the full, making holes not just for feeding, but for constructing roost sites and nest sites, too. Although they can glean insects from the trunk like Treecreepers do, and hack nuts wedged in the bark as Nuthatches can, the ability to excavate sets them apart from their smaller competitors.

Multi-storey

These sorts of micro-habitat distinctions occur throughout the wood. And they don't just apply to the members of winter flocks, but also to the non-social, territorial species. On the ground, for example, both Robins and Blackbirds feed over similar patches of forest floor, but the Blackbird is the one that truly gets stuck in, sifting the leaf-litter and digging in its bill for worms and other submerged goodies. The Robin, by contrast, prefers to perch just above the ground, scanning its patch quietly and waiting for invertebrate food to appear on the woodland floor, whereupon it hops down to snap it up. So one species is pro-active, the other is

more reactive, but they are both ground-feeders. And they are both hotheads, but can share their space because they use it differently.

In a sense, broad-leaved woodland holds more niches for birds than most other habitats. One of the reasons for this is its structure, particularly its vertical structure. Broadly speaking, a wood accommodates four different layers that are differentiated by height: the ground, the field layer, the shrub layer and the canopy. Each of these offers its own suite of opportunities for a bird to meet life's necessities, although no species is entirely confined to any one layer. The Blackbird, for example, usually feeds on the ground, as we have seen, but it builds its nest in the undergrowth – the shrub layer. And Bullfinches, which often feed among the flowers and weeds on the woodland floor, the field layer, are equally adept at using the shrub layer to hide their nest and the canopy for taking meals of buds and tree-flowers.

Another reason for the wide range of niches offered by a wood is its broad species composition. The majority of British deciduous woods comprise many tree species, each of which offers birds distinctive features of its own. Some grow taller than others; some have wider leaves, denser twigs or coarser bark; and some provide more holes for nesting than others. Furthermore, these features each house a suite of associated insect species, which may attract or repel the dis-cerning bird. But perhaps surprisingly, although many bird species have strong preferences for one type of tree or another, the species composition of trees in a wood is much less important to birds than the wood's overall vertical structure.

Bursting out, fitting in

To a visitor, it is during the spring and summer months that the layers of the wood take their clearest shape. It's not just the leaves of the trees that burst out in enthusiastic green at the end of winter; the shrubs of the understorey, such as hazel, often beat them to it, and the show of spring flowers – all fresh blues, whites and yellows – has an

A Blackbird seeks litter bugs.

underlying wash of greenness as the field layer and undergrowth both thicken. Soon the wood is compartmentalised more thoroughly than before; each species locks itself away at its preferred height and becomes a stranger to the others. The Wren, for example, abounds in the field layer and lower shrub layer. But up in the canopy it is as lost as a stray waif, a rarity in its own habitat. Similarly, the Spotted Flycatcher also feeds in the canopy, especially by glades and at the woodland edge, making a living in the fresh, insect-filled air between the treetops. Only in severe weather, rain or high wind, does it go to ground – and grudgingly at that, to wrestle meagre pickings, often downed by the weather. The flycatcher's great gift, of snatching aerial insects, is of no use at ground level.

The flycatcher is only one of many species to tap into the fantastic productivity of the summer woodland canopy. Well above ground, the crowns of trees, all newly in leaf, simply seethe with insects of all kinds throughout the growing season. A single oak tree, for example, may provide a permanent feeding site for 30,000 individual caterpillars – and that's just caterpillars, one single component of a hugely diverse invertebrate fauna. No wonder that birds of all kinds are drawn to the treetops. Blue Tits and Chaffinches can almost disappear for weeks milking this easy food, and birds that you might not expect, such as large-billed, top-heavy Hawfinches and bulky Great Spotted Woodpeckers, contort their bodies so that they, too, can feed up on the abundance in the small branches and outer twigs. The latter, indeed, often cling on to twigs upside down and lap up the insects from the surface of the leaves – hardly the sort of activity we normally associate with these tree-climbing bark bashers.

Not that we can necessarily appreciate all this when we make a visit. Woodland birdwatching in summer can be hard work, made all the more frustrating by the endless disembodied sounds that emanate from behind the green curtain. The richness of a wood, with its nose-to-tail insect traffic and lush, impenetrable undergrowth, is obvious to even the most casual observer. But seeing the birds takes time, effort, silence and a stiff neck, and you will often need to be content with mere glimpses.

And that's exactly how the birds like it – especially when they are sitting on eggs or raising young.

Nest sites

Contrary to what you might expect, only a small minority of woodland birds nest in the canopy; the majority build close to the ground, where the vegetation is usually thicker, and offers more shelter and security. The few that take to the heights are mostly large birds that build substantial nests not easily damaged by high winds. Carrion Crows are a good example, and Grey Herons, too. The latter commute every day to wetland to seek food for their young, making their relationship to the woodland rather like that of weekly digs to a worker: a temporary attachment.

A few smaller birds do nest in the canopy, though. One of the most unlikely of these is surely the Long-tailed Tit. While most pairs of this delicate species sensibly place their nest amidst the security of a spiny bush, a few build very high up, in the fork of a tree. Absolutely none nest at any level in between, a curious polarisation that has never been fully explained. The benefits for this species of canopy nesting are certainly hard to fathom, since the birds usually begin building in

Birds of the woodland strata – the Rook (top) nests in the high canopy, the Chaffinch (middle) gleans summer food from the shrub layer and the Wren (bottom) hugs the ground.

March, when there is little foliage around to conceal them.

About a third of woodland bird species nest in holes or crevices, sites that offer the twin benefits of enhanced shelter and security. In fact, the only major problem with holes is that they tend to be in short supply, and thus can limit the breeding population of a given species. We know this, because when holes are artificially provided, as nest-boxes fitted to trees, some species of bird increase markedly. In the natural state, many individual pairs and even those of different species compete for the same, highly desirable sites, making gazumping, and even direct eviction commonplace. Sometimes even woodpeckers, the main architects of top-end woodland properties, can be thrown out of their own holes by Jackdaws and other voracious house-hunters!

Shaping a wood

Holes and crevices are among the many physical features of a wood that are affected by its management, both past and present. Up until now, somewhat fancifully, we have been considering the structure of a wood in its wild, untouched state, yet only a handful of woods in the whole of Britain fit this blueprint. The rest are products of their exploitation in one form or another by humans, and in reality, the type and number of birds present in a wood ultimately depends more on this than anything else. We have seen how the vertical layers can serve different species in different ways. So when management can promote the growth of one layer, or virtually

remove another, it is not difficult to see that this will have a profound effect on the birdlife.

In many woods in Britain, especially in the upland areas of the west and north, the grazing of sheep beneath the trees effectively eliminates much of the undergrowth in the field and shrub layer. Many of these woods are dominated by Sessile Oaks, and where these trees are allowed to grow to maturity, they hold a highly characteristic set of breeding birds, including Redstarts, Pied Flycatchers and Wood Warblers. The first of these two breed in holes, but the Wood Warbler nests at ground level. One might think that such a bird would shun any wood without much undergrowth, but this fits the Wood Warbler's preference and it thrives there. So the management of the wood directly benefits this species, which can be scarce elsewhere.

Coppicing is another important type of woodland husbandry that strongly affects the bird population. In coppicing, the shoots of certain trees, such as chestnuts and hazels, are regularly harvested for poles and stakes once they have reached a suitable girth, whereupon they re-grow from the stump. The interval between episodes of cutting varies between the tree species, but it is usually about 15 years. As the young trees grow, so the habitat changes, broadly evolving from an open habitat favoured by birds such as Tree Pipits, into deep thickets beloved of Nightingales and Garden Warblers, and finally to a tall stand suitable for the commoner woodland birds such as Chaffinches and Great Tits. In this way it mirrors the natural pattern of regeneration after a wood has been felled.

The management of woodland does not always suit birds. In fact, wherever it reduces the number of layers in a wood, the number of breeding birds falls and so, normally, does the variety of species. Woods in their natural state harbour little corners where mighty trees have fallen and new growth is competing for the space; they also harbour trees of all stages of life, from vigorous saplings to mature giants reaching their end, their edges frayed and some of their limbs dead. Importantly, they accommodate trees that have actually completely died, whose rotting trunks and limbs afford homes to whole communities, including holes for birds.

The dead trees and unproductive corners are usually the first to go when a wood is heavily managed. But this robs the wood of much of its potential life. And then the midwinter dearth of birdlife is no longer an illusion or a tease, but a sad reality.

Woodlands would be much the poorer without the excavating activities of woodpeckers.

A male Pied Flycatcher sings, but he's no choirboy.

Pied Flycatchers as love rats

ONE OF the great things about the curtain of leaves in a summer woodland is that – like curtains everywhere – it offers concealment. Birds can move about and carry on their lives, knowing that prying eyes cannot penetrate the veil of greenery. For most birds, that's all they need and all they want; they require safety and privacy, nothing else.

But there's one woodland bird that uses the concealment of foliage for more than just security. To the Pied Flycatcher leaves offer more than just protection from enemies: they can also hide it from its own kind. As a result, this small bird has more devious uses for its densely growing habitat than mere survival. There are times when being hidden from those you know has distinct advantages.

The Pied Flycatcher is a small migrant bird that is commonest in the verdant Sessile Oak woodland of the west and north of Britain. Here,

in a habitat where food almost drops from the trees, the handsome, black-and-white male takes up a territory and sings his song, somewhat unsubtly, from right above a nesting hole. The song is a gentle ditty that gives the rather odd impression of being played backwards on a tape recorder. But it does its job, and the brown-and-white females, rather taken by the image of a home-loving partner singing from what is effectively a rooftop, are duly beguiled. Soon a pair is formed.

At first all seems well. The birds display and appear inseparable. They chase around skittishly and court frequently to ensure that their chemistry is just right. They also check out other nest holes in case there is better accommodation elsewhere in the male's territory. The male sings with gusto to protect the territory and his family to be. The

101

female lays the clutch of eggs and begins incubation, while her busy partner brings in periodic offerings of food to keep her energy up. If Pied Flycatchers kept photo albums, these would be the days when the pages filled up most quickly with idyllic scenes of domestic bliss.

But the album is a hollow sham. Almost as soon as the female has begun to sit, the offerings of food cease. So does the singing. Anxiously she looks around, seeking her mate. But the search is fruitless: he has gone, never to return. With up to five eggs to look after and bring to chick-hood, the female now faces the exhausting load of the single parent. Her chances of successfully raising the entire brood are, quite honestly, not great, but with persistence she might emerge with one or two young. Meanwhile she is left overworked and abandoned.

Now, if she had been bereaved, her lot could be put down to the sad vagaries of life and death. But she hasn't. She's been conned. Had she learnt from the experience of other female Pied Flycatchers, she might have expected trouble of this kind. But having not paired early in the season, and with her chances of reproducing fading, she has felt compelled to take the plunge. The wrong plunge. This female Pied Flycatcher found herself the victim of a love rat, one of a small but persistent element in the population of male Pied Flycatchers everywhere.

Some female Pied Flycatchers have to feed the young all on their own.

The sad reality for the victim is that her ardent suitor was already paired, leaving her as the unwitting number two in an act of two-timing. In the period that it took for her relationship to develop and produce eggs, the male's first female (the primary female) was already incubating her brood, and his sudden departure will have been triggered by the hatching of this first brood. It would subsequently do the secondary female no good at all to know that, while she was struggling to incubate her eggs and feed her young, her mate will have been giving hearty assistance to his primary female and seeing his primary brood reach maturity. And this secondary female will probably never know, thankfully, that his courting of her was merely a way to increase his own productivity. He would instinctively have known that the secondary female would do all she could to raise his chicks, so he could take the risk in leaving her at incubation, expecting at least a brood and a half from two females for his season's effort.

You're shocked? Actually this is no more than many other birds do, with both sexes often implicated in multiple partnering and cuckoldry. But what is unusual about Pied Flycatcher philandering is the deception involved. In other species – including, for example, Dunnocks and Swallows – the sharing of partners is an open secret. But amongst Pied Flycatchers, there is probably no such expectation of being cheated, and one might assume that the secondary female is genuinely bewildered when her male disappears so suddenly.

Why is this? The reason is proximity. When Dunnocks or Swallows spread their genetic material about, it usually happens within a commune or colony, or at least between near-neighbours. The cheated partner will probably know all the "significant others" involved, and will probably even be close by when the deed happens. But in Pied Flycatchers, the fling will not be with the girl next door; the male may keep his second partner shacked up in a completely different corner of the wood.

The male Pied Flycatcher, you see, practises an unusual system called polyterritoriality, which simply means that he can hold more than one discrete territory at the same time. He will sing to defend one, see his first mate through to the incubation stage, then move to a new territory to sing again, and so on. A few males may hold three territories in the course of a season.

Behind the green curtain of an oakwood, you don't need to move far away to disappear, and this is exactly what the Pied Flycatcher does. No female can keep tabs on him, and this gives him just the kind of freedom he needs.

The cherry pickers

Hawfinches pluck cherries high in the canopy, out of sight.

of the keenest birdwatchers, too. Some of the latter, in fact, swear blind that it doesn't exist, citing some kind of conspiracy. Bless them.

The Hawfinch owes its supreme elusiveness to three main characteristics. First, it is so shy that it takes flight at the slightest provocation – which means that if you so much as step on a stick within half a mile of it, it will be off and away. Second, the Hawfinch is very difficult to hear. It isn't one of those demonstrative finches that cannot stop twittering; instead its occasional calls disappear into the prevailing hubbub, like a nervous question from a novice backbench MP; and its song is stuttering and unmusical – at least to our ears. And the third reason why the Hawfinch is so tricky to find is that it is a bird of the high canopy, almost always hidden by a mass of green leaves. And should it wish to fly from one tree to another, it uses a much higher airspace than other small birds, usually out of sight above the branches.

But although it is elusive, this does not mean that the Hawfinch is unassertive. Any doubters should speak to those hard-working folk who put rings on birds' feet for scientific research. Ask them what it is like to be bitten by a Hawfinch, and they will probably show you the stitches. The Hawfinch is armed with an enormous, conical bill, a tool so massive, and so well served with bulging musculature around the head and neck, that it seems to threaten the owner's balance when perched upright, and almost to drag it down in flight. This bill is a formidable tool that can exert a force of more than 50kg, nine hundred times the bird's own weight and enough to do human fingers very serious damage. It is specially adapted for a tight grip, with two special small knobs on the palate that dig into a food item and help to concentrate the pressure.

So what use is a bill of this sort, since biting researchers – though undoubtedly satisfying –

WHAT IS Britain's most elusive bird? One of the strongest candidates must be the Hawfinch. You've never heard of it? Point proven. You've never seen one? Of course not. The Hawfinch is so difficult to see that, quite honestly, you have a better chance of stumbling across the SAS on exercise than of setting eyes on this large-billed seed-eater. It lives a life of extreme secrecy in the treetops, out of sight of casual observers, and usually out of sight

Don't mess with a Hawfinch.

could only be regarded at best as a fringe activity? The answer is that any wood holds at least a few kinds of seed that can only be tackled with this kind of fearful clenching. Have you ever tried cracking a cherry stone, for example? A Hawfinch can, in six seconds. It is also adept at working hornbeams and elms and, as a sideline, treats sunflower seeds and many other quite robust outfits as mere practice. This is a bird to which no seed, in theory, is off limits – although with its oversized mandibles it does struggle a bit with the very smallest, fiddly ones. The Hawfinch, in short, is at the power end of the seed-cracking continuum.

You might have noticed, however, that the woods of Britain are not densely packed with hornbeams and wild cherries. These are never dominant players among trees, growing flush to make a stand, but are generally dotted about somewhat sparingly. And while it's true that the Hawfinch is quite capable of tackling oak and beech and many other abundant food sources, it is a bird of very particular tastes – sticking faithfully to its favourite foods and therefore allowing its distribution to be dictated by theirs.

And it is not the only one. Finches are a family of birds with made-to-measure bills, and each species tends to be tied to patches of its favourite food plants, (although most can branch out when absolutely necessary). It means that, if you can find the right trees somewhere in sufficient quantity, you can usually find the bird there, too. If you're looking for Bramblings, for example, try a large patch of its favourite seeding beeches; if it's Redpolls you're after, set yourself the tricky task of working through birch clumps; for Siskins – in winter at least – search patches of alder growing among streams; and for Bullfinches, your best bet is ash. Each of these associations reflects millennia of specialisation; as each species has become adept at cracking seeds outside the compass of other species, so competition has become reduced.

And if you can say that each finch is highly selective, then you could also say – metaphorically, at least – that every species, and not just the Hawfinch, is something of a cherry picker.

Separate beds – the curious domestic arrangements of the Chiffchaff

YOU MIGHT not know the Chiffchaff very well, but you will certainly have heard it. Visit any mature wood between late March and July and you will certainly hear it singing its name from the treetops – "*Chiff-chaff, chiff-chaff, chiff-chaff*" – with metronomic monotony. If you look for the source of the sound, you might notice an olive-green, Blue Tit-sized bird on a dead twig above the canopy, throwing its whole body into the effort, a tail-wag for "*chiff*" and a tail-wag for "*chaff*". In fact the scientists say that it is also capable of occasional variations, such as "*chuff*". But, to be honest, this adds little lustre to what, you will probably conclude, is a spirited but somewhat underwhelming song.

If you were unkind, you might describe the singing Chiffchaff as a poor man's Cuckoo. After all, both birds sing their name, both do it from the treetops and both provide a soundtrack for the arrival of spring (the Chiffchaff, indeed, arrives earlier than the Cuckoo). Yet, somehow the Chiffchaff lacks the Cuckoo's star quality. One can imagine the derisory comments from the judges of *Pop Idol* or *The X-Factor*. Next please!

Nevertheless, the Chiffchaff's song certainly resonates for the listeners that matter. It works to delineate the various individual Chiffchaffs'

A Chiffchaff sings full-throttle from a bare twig on a treetop.

territories, and it attracts the females. In short, it does everything that a song is supposed to do; if a Chiffchaff sang anything different, it would achieve none of these required results.

So, cocking a snoop towards our irrelevant opinions, Chiffchaffs go unhindered into the well-worn patterns of reproduction followed by just about every other bird in the wood (except, of course, the Cuckoo). Pairs form and become official; the couple copulates frequently; the female lays an egg each day for a week in the early morning; and then incubation begins. Meanwhile, the male carries on with his highly effective vocalisation – "*Chiff-chaff, chiff…chuff*" – from the canopy. This is vital for maintaining territorial boundaries and asserting his presence in the still strong woodland chorus. (Interestingly, though, he doesn't sing much at dawn – Chiffchaffs are late risers).

So far, you would notice little difference in the Chiffchaff's behaviour from that of most other birds, apart, perhaps, from the monotony of its song. But there is a difference. The more you watch, the more you realise that the two partners in a Chiffchaff relationship seem to co-operate with each other very little, even in the most basic tasks. As the breeding season goes on, the more their pair bond begins to resemble that of a deteriorating marriage.

The male Chiffchaff, you see, is a bit more of a slob than most other small birds. He doesn't help build the nest – although, like many small species, he may sit back and watch the work being done. Less typically, he rarely if ever delivers a bill-full of food for his hard-pressed mate; this so-called "courtship-feeding" is a staple for many species, helping females to nourish themselves while they are forming eggs inside. Even more strangely, he hardly ever visits the female when she is incubating the eggs. And as for helping to feed the chicks, no way! Effectively, the pair bond between the two breeding partners is severed completely by the time of incubation.

In the majority of small birds, the male does help to feed the chicks, if little else. Even males with several mates tend to lend a hand to at least one of their families. Thus the male Chiffchaff's abstention from parenting duties is unusual, and rather puzzling. Sure, within the abundance of the woodland leaves the female can usually find enough food to bring the chicks up by herself. So could many other birds in this richest of summer habitats, but they don't usually need to cope without a contribution from their mate.

Still more peculiar is the effective spatial separation between a male and female Chiffchaff that lasts throughout the breeding season. It is

perfectly possible for the two partners never to cross paths for the course of an entire day. This is because they partition their territory between themselves as though they were separate species. The male Chiffchaff is very much a bird of the canopy, spending virtually all his time feeding and singing high above ground. The female, on

Early arrivals in the spring, Chiffchaffs often seek insects among the first blooms of willow.

the other hand, is a denizen of the understorey and shrub layer. The nest, too, is always placed on or close to the ground, hidden by tall vegetation. It is quite possible that birdwatchers in woodland rarely come across female Chiffchaffs, because of this bird's secretive, low-level existence.

If a broad-leafed wood were a house, then the living quarters of male and female Chiffchaffs would effectively be on different floors, the female taking the ground floor and the male inhabiting the attic and roof. For a male Chiffchaff, it takes a conscious choice to visit his mate and to enter her world, which is quite different from his. And he does so from time to time, but so seldom that the sexes effectively live apart – their lives separated by an invisible ceiling.

I'm not for a moment suggesting a genuine theory on why a pair of Chiffchaffs should sleep in separate beds. I do know one thing, though: if I had to live on a desert island listening to a Chiffchaff singing all day, it wouldn't be long before I wanted to throttle it. But surely escaping that relentlessly dreary song couldn't possibly be a motive for one bird to avoid its partner.

Or could it?

EVERGREEN
FORESTS

Needles in haystacks

THE WORD "evergreen" is not really the right description for coniferous forests. It's a bit too cheery. These woods are green alright, but it's definitely a dark, muted version of the colour. In the same way, the birdlife of a coniferous wood is also somewhat muted and modest. There are special birds here, but they are thinly spread and hard to find.

ON THE face of it, the lack of birds in Britain's coniferous woodlands is a paradox. The needles ought to teem with birds. By keeping their leaves through the winter conifers offer food and shelter on a year-round basis, which is something that the seasonally denuded broad-leaved woodlands cannot do. Conifers also produce a healthy seed crop in season, just as deciduous trees do, and conifers are often found in large stands which lack the fragmented nature of many of our broad-leaved woods. These advantages should make them an exceedingly rich habitat, the sort that birdwatchers flock to rather than avoid.

But things are not always so simple. Many birdwatching trips into conifer woods are fruitless and frustrating. Even in the heart of the richest pinewoods in the country, those found in the Highlands, there can still be a penetrating stillness and silence that is rarely encountered even in the most abused and battered deciduous woods down south. No, there is clearly something at the heart of conifers that makes them relatively unattractive to birds.

There are several reasons why, in Britain, conifer stands are not as bird-rich as broad-leaved woods. One is that there are almost invariably fewer species of trees in a conifer stand, which means less variety in the woodland structure (including fewer small trees and thick branches) and, consequently, a smaller variety of available food items and ecological niches. Most British deciduous woods are full of different species of plant, but this is not the case with conifers. The reason behind the difference, of course, is that most British conifer stands are actually plantations, created by people for commercial gain. So you could look at them as very large fields, all planted with the same crop. No wonder they hold little interest for birds.

These difficulties are compounded by the fact that a good many of the coniferous trees planted in Britain are not native, and therefore they are

Previous spread: Capercaillies in the snow.

not especially popular with the local insects. Each of our native trees, from birches and oaks to alders and elms, has its own special suite of invertebrates that has grown up alongside it and for which it becomes a micro-habitat. But Britain only has three native conifers – the Scots Pine, the Yew and the Juniper, and the latter is really a shrub. Foreign imports simply cannot match their home-grown ecological benefits, and although a good many insects do use the introduced trees, they are inevitably in the minority, and consequently the bird diversity is impoverished.

Finally, conifers, on the whole, are not very friendly towards the understorey – that low layer of growth where, in other kinds of woodland, a good many birds flourish. We've all tramped through plantations of wall-to-wall evergreens; they can be dark, forbidding, sterile places, with nothing growing at our feet. And to some extent, almost all conifers have a habit of shutting out the light below them, simply by the thickness of the foliage on their crowns. Again, this has the effect of reducing the variety within the wood, confining many birds to the upper stratum, the canopy. However, the natural pinewoods in the north of Scotland and elsewhere are not like this; the trees are well spaced, with a rich herb layer of plants such as bilberries growing below them, which in season are highly attractive to birds.

Specialists

Despite their relative avian impoverishment, it would be quite wrong to write off conifer woods as an abomination on the land. There are birds to be found here, sometimes in good numbers and in reasonable variety. Evergreens have the added attraction of hosting specialists that simply do not occur anywhere else, which makes them popular with birdwatchers in search of unusual species. Indeed, many feathered coniferous inhabitants are more closely tied to their specific habitat than the equivalent larger guild of broad-leaved foragers. We can draw an analogy to football supporters here: the devoted followers of an impecunious home-town club are less likely to switch their allegiance than the fickle followers of a large, successful outfit. Conifer specialists, therefore, are in it for life.

So what exactly do conifers offer? The first and most obvious feature is their dense growth of needles, which offers excellent shelter. In the winter many birds come to conifers just for the night, taking advantage of the copious foliage, even if they do not normally visit for food during the

day. Several species of finch, such as Greenfinches, Chaffinches, Bramblings and Bullfinches are nightly tenants, as are some thrushes and – occasionally – crows. It is easy to see why they come, especially when the leaves have fallen from the broad-leaved trees.

Britain's answer to the hummingbird – a Goldcrest hovers to pick insects off the needle ends.

A relatively small number of species use the needled foliage for foraging purposes, primarily because it is not very easy to work. Britain's commonest conifer-loving tit, the Coal Tit, has a very small body and a thin bill, which are vital for investigating the confined spaces between needles where minute insects hide on stems and leaves. The Goldcrest and Firecrest, smaller birds still, also forage here in the same way and – as if to demonstrate what a difficult task they must accomplish – these birds hover much more frequently than other small birds, which is often the only way they can reach food at the end of coniferous stems. On the plus side, having mastered this skill, they face little competition from other species, and thrive as a result.

Only two birds regularly consume the needles themselves, and both of these are members of the grouse family: the Capercaillie, which occurs in just a few forests in the Highlands, and the more wide-ranging Black Grouse. Conifer needles don't look very tempting, and they are not especially nutritious; the birds have to consume them in large quantities to get any benefit from them and, of the two

The diminutive Coal Tit is a conifer specialist.

109

species, only the Capercaillie "treats" itself to many at all.

The seeds of conifers, however, are much better fare, and they are harvested by a significant number of bird species. Some of these, such as Treecreepers and Great Spotted Woodpeckers, are wide-ranging birds that include these woodlands within a wider portfolio. The Treecreeper, which feeds primarily on insects, also eats the minute seeds of spruce, but usually ignores plant produce from deciduous trees. The Great Spotted Woodpecker, on the other hand, is very much an omnivore wherever it occurs. It winkles out the insect life on evergreen trunks and branches throughout the year, and takes huge quantities of seeds in autumn. With its powerful bill, it can easily demolish the scales of pine cones and guzzle seeds to its heart's content. In fact, Great Spotted Woodpeckers do well in this habitat. These birds often have special "anvils" within their territory, places where they can lodge a cone between tough bits of wood and hack it open. The astute human observer who finds piles of spent cones below one of these work-stations can deduce immediately what goes on in the branches above.

Signs

Another treetop feeder also leaves telltale signs beneath it. This is the Crossbill, a large finch with a bill specially adapted for extracting seeds from between the scales of pine and spruce cones. Crossbills also break cones off their stems and it is possible, by careful examination of the fallen cones below the tree, to tell which bird it is that has been working upon them. The woodpecker, for instance, leaves piles of cones, whereas Crossbills drop theirs over a wider area. And the cones ransacked by Woodpeckers are often worked only on one side, many showing split scales, rough edges and broken ends. The Crossbill's work, by contrast, is much more precise and thorough: most of the scales remain in situ, but they are all split neatly down the middle and forced outwards, leaving gaping gaps where they used to lie flush to each other. If you find such a cone, it is always worth looking upwards. These birds habitually feed

in near silence and it's quite possible that you might have missed a sizeable flock above you, all munching away.

Most of the Crossbills found in Britain belong to a clan that specialises in extracting spruce seeds, and in autumn also visit larches for a little variety. In the Highlands, however, where our own special form of native Scots Pine grows, there are Crossbills with broader bills than the rest that are entirely dependent on these native trees all year round. They also have slightly different calls from Common Crossbills, and the general consensus is that they probably constitute a distinct species. If so then, significantly, this makes them the one and only bird species that is confined to Britain; all our other birds occur elsewhere on the continent. If it wasn't so similar to the Common Crossbill – so much so that hardly anyone can identify it – the Scottish Crossbill would have gained quite an iconic status by now.

The Siskin is another finch that visits conifer forests for their seeds. This bird's bill is much thinner than that of the Crossbill and this means that, unlike its relative, it must always wait for the cone to open up before it can reach in. But thin bills have their advantages: Siskins can probe into much smaller spaces than Crossbills and the bill's two mandibles can act rather like a pair of tweezers. The muscle opening the bill is much more powerful than the one closing it – an arrangement that is the reverse of our own – and this means that the Siskin can make small entrances larger, which is very useful when foraging among opening cones. The Siskin is primarily a spruce specialist, so many hundreds of years ago, before this tree was introduced, it must have been quite scarce in Britain. Nowadays, however, with spruce widely sown in plantations, this attractive yellow-green finch is already found over much of the country and is still spreading fast.

Of course there is more to conifers than just needles and seeds, and a good many birds utilise many different parts of the trees. The Crested Tit, for example, feeds on seeds in the autumn and winter, which it gets from the cones or on the ground, and on

A Great Spotted Woodpecker hacks at a cone lodged in the bark – it is after the seeds embedded within.

The thin bill of the Siskin is adapted for prising open the scales of cones.

insects and spiders in the spring and summer, which abound in the canopy and along boughs and branches. In the spring, furthermore, it carries out an unusual operation for a small bird: it excavates its own nest-hole, like a mini-Woodpecker. Not surprisingly, for a tiny bird with a strong but undeniably small bill, it favours soft or rotting bark for this operation, so it is often drawn to decaying tree stumps – yet another commodity available within the forest.

Rarities and commoners

The Crested Tit, despite its apparent adaptability within the habitat, is a very rare bird indeed in Britain. It only occurs in the natural pinewoods and nearby plantations of the central part of Scotland, and is virtually never seen anywhere else. In contrast to our more familiar tits, this bird is not very sociable; it sticks to its territory for a lifetime, instead of joining other birds to roam around in the autumn. Perhaps this is one reason why, despite there now being suitable habitat available in England, it has not yet spread down south.

Although both Crested Tits and Coal Tits are the archetypal tits of coniferous woodland, always choosing this habitat for their breeding sites, other members of their family are also sometimes found among the needles. Blue Tits and, especially, Great Tits often share the canopy with their less forceful relatives, although they never reach the abundance here that they do in the broad-leaved woodlands. The obvious reason is that the coniferous canopy – by contrast with, say, oakwoods – just doesn't quite drip with caterpillar food in the same way, so it is harder to make a living and feed the chicks. To these species, therefore, coniferous stands are really sub-optimal habitat, the home – to be brutally frank – of substandard individuals who are unable to hold territories among better foliage. For these species conifer woods are merely economy class dwellings, where you venture only if you must.

The Crested Tit is one of the few British birds exclusively confined to coniferous woodland.

A good many other common birds can also be found at lower density hereabouts than in their core habitat. For example, Robins, Blackbirds, Wrens, Woodpigeons and Willow Warblers take to the shrub layer, the ground, the undergrowth and the treetops of coniferous woodlands, but never quite in the numbers that would suggest that they truly thrive here. There are exceptions, though. If you walk through some conifer stands, especially in Scotland, you hear the rattling song of the Chaffinch more than anything else – at times, it seems, from every treetop. This species, at least, seems to have the measure of just about every type of woodland.

At the very top of the food-chain in some British conifer forests perches the formidable Goshawk. This is a terrifying predator. It hunts primarily by stealth, spending much of its time hidden in the dense foliage before launching surprise attacks on its victims, which may be as large as woodpigeons and even squirrels. Compared to its more common cousin, the Sparrowhawk, the Goshawk is huge. (Indeed, its tummy is big enough to accommodate a Sparrowhawk, and sometimes does.) It is a fast, secretive and ruthless killer and – happily for many forest animals – one that is still largely restricted to conifers, which offer the seclusion it craves.

The Goshawk was once a great rarity in Britain; in fact, it was probably extinct between the late nineteenth century and the middle of the twentieth, destroyed by persecution and the gamekeeper's gun. But then groups of birds were

Nightmare in the treetops – a Goshawk snatches a Red Squirrel.

deliberately released in several parts of the country by eager falconers. Having been reintroduced to their former haunts, Goshawks have subsequently thrived, and there are now at least 400 pairs of this powerful predator at large in our countryside.

The success of the Goshawk mirrors that of several other coniferous forest species. They have each expanded their range as, little by little, the amount of land covered by forest has also increased – mainly due to the spread of commercial forestry. Although the planting of evergreen forests has now slowed down, birds such as Siskins and Goldcrests are much commoner than they once were, and the change is certainly a long-term one. And, who knows, perhaps one day this sort of change will be wholesale and a trip to a conifer stand will be a much more exciting, bird-filled affair than it is today?

Slaves to seeds

WHEN CROSSBILLS first developed a special way to open the cones of conifer seeds, they must have thought they had hit the jackpot. Suddenly a whole new world had opened up, untapped by any other bird. By being able to reach into the ripening cones of spruces and pines, they would be feasting on a resource virtually free of competitors. How many species can ever say that? Billions upon billions of food items would be theirs alone. Crossbills would take over the world!

Well, they were right, in a way. But what they didn't realise was that, over time, they were also doomed to slavery. Being seed specialists in this way would take over every aspect of their lives. They could no longer breed as other birds do, moult as other birds do, or travel in regular patterns like other birds do. They would reproduce when the seeds told them and travel as the seeds told them. Their lives would no longer be their own: instead they were about to become serfs in the great kingdom of the evergreen forests, with no hope of escape.

You may well have never heard of a Crossbill, let alone seen one. That's probably because these highly specialised finches hang out deep in large coniferous woodlands and forests. But if you ever chanced upon their picture in the pages of a bird book, you would recognise immediately that they were something special. For the bizarre feature that gives them their name is unique in the bird world: their bill is crossed – or rather, its mandibles are. A Crossbill cannot shut its bill without part of one mandible lying alongside, instead of on top of, the other.

Technically it is the lower mandible that passes to the side of the upper one. When young Crossbills hatch, their bills are like those of normal birds, and it is only after 27 days that the twist begins to show. And interestingly, the bill may twist either to the right or to the left; Crossbills are left-billed or right-billed, just as we are left- or right-handed.

The crossing of the mandibles is an adaptation for opening recalcitrant cones that have not yet ripened enough to be released by the tree. They

Feeding on cones has its ups and downs.

are still protected by hard scales, shut tight as barnacles. To breach the defences, the Crossbill simply pokes its opened bill between two scales and then closes its mouth. This act of closing the bill – which, with crossed mandibles, increases its width – forces the scales apart. The bird can now slightly open its bill again and scoop the seeds out with its tongue. Sounds simple, but only if – like the Crossbill – you have the tool for the job.

Of course, a specialised tool is often great for its specific task, but lousy for anything else. You wouldn't, for example, try peeling carrots with a corkscrew. The Crossbill is pretty hopeless at opening other plant seeds, although it can get by in extreme circumstances by working hard at thistles, for example. But the truth is, it cannot survive for long without finding cones in the pre-ripe or ripe stage.

And that, for the Crossbill, is a huge problem. Spruces, its favourite trees, are not very good benefactors. Indeed, they are thoroughly awkward. They never seem to produce a good crop of seeds from one year to the next, and this malaise can be concurrent over a wide area. In a bad season, if the seeds cannot sustain the population, the Crossbills must move out or die. And there is a word for this state of affairs: Crossbills are nomadic. They must travel from place to place following what are often unpredictable food supplies. They may disappear from a locality for many years, only to return

A female Crossbill. This bird's lower mandible crosses to the right of the upper, but individuals can be either right- or left-billed.

113

again, several generations later. They have no "home" and they do not have a standard migration. Their ticket is always one-way.

The availability of ripening seeds also dictates when Crossbills breed. Since their young are entirely dependent on healthy seed supplies, the birds are obliged to reproduce when seed production is at its highest and that, inconveniently enough, is often in the very middle of winter. Those Crossbills found in England, for example, which often feed on planted pines, may find themselves having to incubate eggs in January or February. Needless to say, it can be bitingly cold at such a time, especially in the draughty treetops where these birds construct their nests. There is a famous record of a Crossbill being found on a nest near Moscow where the external temperature was −19°C. The scientists also recorded the temperature beneath the bird itself, at the brood patch where the eggs were heated by the skin, and found it be to +38°C, a remarkable 57 degrees warmer than the outside. It takes a lot of internal fuel to do that.

The moult, that annual replacement of worn out feathers, must also take place when the food supply is assured. Moulting is a process that demands a lot of energy, a little like adolescence, and requires a similar amount of fuel (though not junk food). The Crossbills are obliged, therefore, to moult at these absurdly chilly times of year. On occasion, they will actually moult at the same time as breeding, making them one of very few birds in the world to carry out these two tasks at once.

Despite these inconveniences, the Crossbill is undoubtedly a highly successful species. Its design is unique and, therefore, its "career development" has been equally so. It copes with many problems that would defeat other birds, and lives at an abundance – albeit highly localised – that many other species would envy. Its habitat is also one of the largest, in surface area, of any bird species in the world, giving the Crossbill a potential buffer against habitat destruction and some of the many other human activities that routinely threaten other such specialised birds. So, in a sense, the slavery to seeds has worked in the Crossbill's favour.

Even so, if a Crossbill ever wanted to uncross, its path has been well and truly blocked.

A bit of needle

Up in the Highlands we somehow expect to find monsters. There is an awful lot of forest in those parts, we argue, where a large animal might hide, and those people who might find it are thinly

Capercaillies can be hard to spot in the thick coniferous canopy.

scattered. In some remote corner, in a hidden glen where no one goes, we fancifully suppose that there just might be something dangerous. The Loch Ness Monster has faded away into the mists of legend, and the big cats supposedly at large are not performing persuasively. But surely there is something there?

Well actually, there is. It might not live up to our idea of a monster, and it has too many feathers to do you any serious harm. But its credentials are not bad. It does, after all, regularly attack people and – close up – it can be quite terrifying.

The monster in question is a large member of the grouse family called the Capercaillie. It is only found in Highland conifer forests with a generous understorey of heathy plants that produce berries in the summer and autumn. In the winter, Capercaillies live a life of unrelenting tedium and so, perhaps not surprisingly, when the early spring finally uncorks a bit of life, they go wildly over the top – like squaddies unleashed from a stint in an alcohol-free country.

The winter really is a trying time for a vigorous, passionate grouse. Once the berry crop is spent, there isn't much to eat. In fact, almost nothing at all. So the Capercaillies reluctantly fly up to the treetops, take a deep breath, and endure the entire cold season nibbling on almost nothing but pine needles. These are not especially nutritious, but there are, let's face it, plenty of them. Capercaillies have long guts and nothing much to do, so they digest their food very slowly and their alimentary canal squeezes out everything it can. Needles must be pretty uncomfortable to eat, and who knows whether the birds can taste them? But that, regrettably, is the Capercaillie's lot. At least the forest canopy is dripping with this food, and offers a good place for these turkey-sized birds to hide away from predators.

Nonetheless, when Capercaillies do finally emerge from the trees, they are in a pretty tetchy mood. They are also mad with lust, and that combination tends to make them unpredictable, rash and – quite frankly – well worth avoiding.

Their breeding system hardly helps. The pair-bond between male and female is based purely on sex, with the birds only meeting for the purposes of copulation. So there is nothing to civilise the males; instead they all compete against each other for these brief flings, in a sort of winner-takes-all arrangement that gives all the sexual pickings to the dominant birds. Worst still, the males tend to display within sight of each other and so, when the females are in the mood for copulation, they are able to watch all the talent displaying and pick out the performer that takes their fancy. In full sight of all, the females ignore the best efforts of the subordinates and trot straight over to where the top males are strutting their stuff. It must double the frustration of the losers when the winners get together so publicly.

Not surprisingly, this situation leaves a good number of birds very cross indeed. The subordinates are furious because they cannot impress and, therefore, impregnate a female. Meanwhile, the dominant birds appear furious, whether or not they actually are, because this is what they do best. Their aggression is all testosterone-induced showing off, with – no doubt – an inner glow of delight helping to fuel it.

But, for whatever reason, everybody is fuming, and there's nothing like an atmosphere of aggression to spark off arguments. Within the forest at Capercaillie mating time, the air is thick with needle, in every sense. Each morning the males awake well before dawn and begin to display immediately. After a brief sing-song in the treetops, during which they may pace back and forth along a thick branch, they flutter to the ground and assume an upright posture, with their head pointing to the sky. Here they ruffle their throat feathers, droop their wing feathers and fan their tail-feathers like cut-price peacocks, before making little forward paces, a bit like cartoon soldiers, while uttering a strange sound like the popping of a champagne cork. They also flutter their wings and jump into the air.

These displays continue until, as inevitably

'What are you looking at?'

happens, there is a confrontation. A nearby male invariably takes umbrage at his rival's show of force and, like two members of a street gang fighting for "respect", the two birds are soon facing off for a scrap. There might be a brief lull while they assess their chances, but the tinder is lit when first one, then the other, belches loudly straight in his rival's face. This sound, which is similar to the rutting call of a deer, is basically an insult.

Capercaillie fights often don't look particularly vicious. There isn't much blood, but there are casualties. Birds regularly die from their injuries, despite the fact that, as an offensive weapon, only the bill, and not the powerful legs, is used. Nevertheless, the combatants grapple fiercely with each other, aiming vicious pecks at the eyes and head. The striking of bill on bill may resound for some distance, like the clashing of deer horns. There is much commotion, and the birds can be so absorbed that they step on, or trip over, their own wing-feathers. Fights may last for quite some time and – in a curious parallel with organised human combat – there may be "rounds", with pauses in between, each bird taking a moment to catch breath. At the end of battles between well-matched birds, both winner and loser may become so exhausted that they can hardly, one suspects, muster a belch.

Now it is into this battleground that bystanders occasionally stray.

Human brawls often claim innocent victims, and Capercaillie skirmishes are no different. Any deer or sheep that blunders onto the battlefield becomes fair game. Even humans have been set upon: hikers, mountaineers and cyclists have all felt the ire of the big bird. And photographers, loaded with gear to record the scene, have become the scene; some even have the scars to prove it. Now this might all seem fairly amusing, but a rampaging Capercaillie is big, aggressive and very quick. If you do stumble across a fight, you would be well advised to beat a retreat. This is one Highlands monster that really might get you.

The Goldcrest's draught-proof nest

YOU MAY not have heard of the Goldcrest, but it has the distinction of being the smallest bird in Britain, smaller even than a Wren – and definitely more demure, with only half of the Wren's over-cooked effervescence. In the winter it lives all over the place, including gardens, yet its diminutive size and avoidance of bird feeders means that people don't always notice it, and it is not a trilling loudmouth like the Wren, so they don't easily hear it either. In the breeding season it withdraws to its favourite habitat, coniferous woodland and forest, disappearing into the vastness of the needles so you need never know that it existed at all. But here, nonetheless, it abounds, being often the most numerous bird in the entire habitat.

Clearly there are advantages to being small. Goldcrests are only rarely attacked by Sparrowhawks and other predatory birds, probably for the very obvious reason that they do not make a very substantial meal – certainly not worth the effort of catching. They are also difficult to spot, and live at low densities. Being small also allows Goldcrests to penetrate deeper among the needles of conifers than almost all other birds, tapping into a rich source of tiny food items beyond the reach of almost every competitor. Being small has made Goldcrests successful.

But there are also disadvantages to being downsized. With their high surface-area-to-volume ratio, small birds lose heat more rapidly than larger ones, meaning that Goldcrests have difficulty surviving in cold conditions without feeding literally all day long in order to keep their internal fires stoked. And when they roost at night, Goldcrests are often forced to huddle together for warmth, like stranded mountaineers. Huddling is stressful, as it eliminates personal space and may pass on disease or parasites. But Goldcrests muck through, and enough survive each winter to keep the population high, despite the difficulties.

In April, when they begin to breed, Goldcrests face another difficulty.

Falls of snow need not be a disaster for the resilient Goldcrest.

They might be small themselves, but their young are even smaller, and even more vulnerable to the cold than their parents are. And incubation and brooding duties force the parents to sit still, which they are not accustomed to doing, and prevent them from feeding and keeping fuelled. All in all, the necessity of breeding exposes Goldcrests to further peril from the chill, especially on those colder nights that the spring and summer may dump upon the forest – especially in the north of Scotland.

So Goldcrests have, over the millennia, paid very careful attention to how they build their nests. Their constructions are more intricate than those of most other small birds, and take longer to build – up to 20 days. Everything about them – where they are sited, what they are made of and their physical structure – serves a purpose. Thus the nests we see today, representing the culmination of trial and error in generations of Goldcrests, are well-insulated, strong and carefully hidden among the needles.

Sites for Goldcrest nests vary greatly in height above ground, from just a metre or so, to 14 or 15 metres, depending on the trees in which they are built. Fundamentally, though, they are always hidden among thick foliage for cover and usually placed towards the end of branches. This location

might leave them to sway along with the wind a little, but even this problem is minimised – the Goldcrest having a canny habit of building on the opposite side of a tree from the prevailing local gusts.

Goldcrests start the construction work by seeking out a rather unusual ingredient – cobwebs. Unlike the majority of small birds' nests, which are cups built on top of branches or twigs, Goldcrest nests are suspended sacs, and must therefore first be anchored to their point of attachment. So the birds collect cobwebs and string them between twigs to form a support structure, and only when they have something of a canopy do they start work on the rest of the nest.

The next phase also involves spider silk. The aim is to create an outer casing, suspended like a hanging basket, so that two layers of insulating material can be placed within. The basic building blocks of the outer casing are fragments of lichen and moss, and these are fastened together with cobwebs, which work like "mortar" to the "bricks" of moss or lichen. The resulting sac is dense and insulating, and – being made out of local materials – fits unobtrusively into its surroundings.

The rest of the building process is all about adding insulating layers. Flush to the outer casing the birds fit in a layer of moss and lichen, unwoven by spider's webs, and then, finally, they collect small feathers and hair from their neighbourhood to make the nest cup itself warm and snug.

Yet the most interesting aspect of this intricate nest is in its overall physical dimensions and placing, which show special, yet subtle adaptations to cold climates. For example, the top of the Goldcrest's suspended sac, where the entrance is sited, is placed very close to the branch from which it hangs. This must be maddening to the birds, because every time they visit they have to squeeze between the branch and the entrance to

A Goldcrest checks the insulation.

get in, but it ensures that the passage of cold air is blocked. And the upper rim of the nest is itself distinctly narrow, no wider than the birds themselves, for the very same reason.

But the neatest adaptation, and the most unusual, is another feature of the nest rim. When the birds have nearly completed the nest, they seek out feathers that are somewhat larger than those used to line the cup. These they then fit into the rim, with the bare shafts facing upward and outward, and the wide, soft ends of the feathers facing down, into the nest. Both sides of the rim are so fitted, and the result is a curtain of plumage that screens the entrance, through which the birds have to pass in order to reach the nest chamber.

This curtain is another protection against the chill outside, restricting the flow of air. No matter what the weather might be, inside their nest the Goldcrests are immune to it all.

ESTUARIES

The ebb and the flow

THE ESTUARY is not a single habitat, but really two of them, job-sharing. At high tide all you can see is an inlet of shallow sea; at low tide, a landscape of flat mud broken up by creeks and channels lies before you. At any given time the water is about to replace the mud, or vice versa. In this dynamic system, the birds can never afford to stay still for long.

ESTUARIES FORM where rivers reach the sea and their flow is abruptly stilled. At this point, the water deposits all the silt it has gathered on its way down, since the current no longer has enough momentum to carry it along. This silt piles up to the point where it lies just below the surface and is exposed at low tide. Thus is created the intertidal zone, a new and ephemeral habitat that exists between low and high water.

The mud of the intertidal zone is fantastically productive. It might look treacherous and bleak to us, but it is a banqueting suite to birds. The fertile ooze plays host to countless millions of small animals living just below the surface. To give one example: the Redshank's favourite food, a tiny shrimp-like creature called *Corophium volutator*, can in places be found at a density of 6,000 individuals per square metre of mud. In all, that same square metre may offer 22,000 edible items of various sorts, all available to grateful bills.

The intertidal zone, then, offers plenty of food to its visitors. But not all that food is the same: different comestibles occur in different areas and at different depths in the mud. Cockles, for example, stay buried deep down, while their fellow shellfish, the mussels, appear at the surface in banks very close to the low water mark.

Each of the various species of worm that inhabit the ooze burrows down to a different level. The same applies to the third main category of food found in an estuary, the crustaceans: some live in the mud; others hop along the surface of drier sand and seaweed further up towards the high water mark. So not only does the estuary provide plenty, it provides variety, too.

And the supply is not cut off at high tide, when the estuary becomes a shallow sea. Although the mud is covered by water, a good many estuarine birds are swimmers and can each find food in their differing ways. Ducks and cormorants, for example, chase fish in the shallows, while gulls paddle about and snatch morsels from the water surface – at their feet, so to speak. Specialists such as Eiders dive down to the mussel beds and catch the unsuspecting molluscs as they idly filter-feed. Shelducks are consummate experts in intertidal life: they dabble over exposed mud at low tide; immerse their head and neck as the mud is covered by shallow water; and then up-end when the water gets deeper, so that their tail points up and their head down, allowing their long necks to reach the muddy bottom. Not all of these birds are exclusively intertidal feeders, but they are, of course, foraging over the very same area as the true mud-lovers.

It is hard to over-emphasise the dynamic nature of an estuary, and not just the way it changes from tide to tide. The constant movement of water continually washes and enriches the mud, and the river keeps adding more silt. Whilst this ensures that the estuary remains productive, it also keeps moving the goalposts for the birds, making different parts of the estuary the most productive at different times. To make things even more complicated and capricious, the tide's height varies according to the lunar cycle and the weather.

So, to make the most of the intertidal plenty, a bird needs to be flexible and resourceful – the best deals come and go, and the market must be followed closely. The birds, therefore, move around in search of optimum conditions. Many prefer to feed at the point where the tide is receding and uncovering the mud-living organisms afresh; others prefer drier mud, where more creatures actually crawl across the surface. Whatever its preference, though, each bird must keep on the move; nothing stays the same.

Stop…run…peck

The activity on an estuary reaches its peak in the cold months of the year, when, without any breeding responsibilities, the birds can concentrate simply on feeding. If you visit at the beginning of a rising tide, perhaps on a January day when the wind is not too sharp, you can spend time watching the estuary's inhabitants and appreciate the change in shifts as the water encroaches. At first, with the water far away, you will see just mud, slimy near the edge of the creeks, harder and sandier in parts and, in others, encrusted with salt-marsh grass. Here, near the high water mark, things have a sedate feel, and you might suspect at first that there is little going on. But get your eye in, and you will probably notice a dusting of gulls over the grey mud, their white bodies just standing out as they loaf, motionless, head tucked away, waiting out the hours before they can get their feet wet. Look more closely and you will almost certainly begin to pick out darker birds that are not resting, but working the mud methodically. They wander over the surface with an industrious, but not frenetic air. These are waders, and members of one of the estuary's two major guilds: the sight-feeders.

Towards the high tide line the mud becomes more compact, so the surface is the easiest part for a foraging bird to work; and with salt-marsh, sand or even shingle nearby, there are often plenty of places for creatures to hide without burrowing into the substrate. Here, far from water, the Turnstone makes a living by doing what its name suggests, overturning stones and other objects to see what is underneath – just like a curious child searching for creepy-crawlies. This Starling-sized bird has a short but very strong bill, ideal for thrusting matter aside with a flip of its muscular neck before

A Turnstone uses its short, sharp bill to deal with a mussel.

grabbing the goodies revealed underneath. Turnstones frequently work in small groups, and will at times pool their resources to lift a very heavy but promising item with a simultaneous "bills-up" heave. The technique is unchanging but the rewards can be surprising. Turnstones have a famously wide diet, and have been known to tuck into anything from bars of soap to human corpses.

The exposed mud itself can also offer good hunting areas. If a bird knows how to read the signs, the apparently lifeless surface is packed with food. For example, ragworms live in tunnels several centimetres down, but every so often they must raise their rear end to the surface to defecate. The worm's act of excreting its cast makes a small movement in the mud, just enough to catch the eye of a vigilant bird. Thus, with its metaphorical trousers down, the poor ragworm meets a sorry end.

Sight-feeders succeed only by careful vigilance. They could run about at random and pick up whatever they come across, but this method would not be very effective, because the food they sought would usually see or feel their approach from some distance away. Instead, most employ a more calculating method. Typically, they begin their search by standing completely still and scanning the mud; then, if nothing comes into view, they scurry a few paces to a new observation point to scan from there; if nothing moves they will move along to another position nearby, and so on. If during this reconnaissance they spy something, they dash towards the food source and grab it with a peck. So this operation, a stop-start method of feeding which is essentially the same technique a Blackbird uses to catch worms on your garden lawn, makes the sight-feeders stand out from other birds. It is known as stop-run-peck.

A worm makes a welcome change from hard-shelled invertebrates for this Grey Plover.

On an estuary the main stop-run-peckers are the plovers, especially the Ringed Plover and the Grey Plover.

Not surprisingly, the sight-feeders tend to have short bills. They are working the surface, so their catching apparatus has more need for strength than reach. But there are exceptions, and one of the more surprising is a bird with a supremely long bill, the Curlew. This distinctive straw-coloured wader is by far our largest. It uses its long legs to walk over the salt-marsh and peer down for food, and the bill is curved in such a way that the Curlew can comfortably pick prey such as crabs straight from the surface. This bird, indeed, has the best of both worlds: besides its surface operations it can also probe deeper than most other waders, so it is highly proficient at obtaining food from both above and below the muddy surface.

Stitch and probe

If you continue your vigil as the tide starts coming in, you will soon notice the tempo in the intertidal zone picking up pace. Instead of the gentle, rhythmic movement induced by the sight-feeders,

the mood will be overtaken by a more rapid, non-stop style of foraging; that of the touch-feeders. Indeed, as the tide creeps towards its highest point, so the scene will become more and more frenetic, the birds working the last of the exposed mud before it is completely covered by water. The bustle can look like the approach of Christmas at a shopping centre, where, as the clock ticks down, the movements of the shoppers speed up, becoming less considered and more instinctive. In the end, what mud is left is covered by a seething muddle of probing bills.

But despite appearances, touch feeding is highly effective. The density of organisms in estuarine mud is such that, in places, almost any probe of the bill can make a strike. And besides, the birds that feed in tactile ways, which are mostly waders, have such highly sophisticated detection apparatus that they don't need to rely on anything like chance. The tips of their probing bills are fitted with many millions of sensory receptors, which give them phenomenal touch sensitivity, at least equivalent to that of the tips of our fingers and on a much smaller scale. In fact, one suspects that they can find prey pretty easily. Sanderlings, for instance, don't even need to touch particles to determine that they are present; they can detect the minuscule vibrations of worms in the substrate instead, even when these worms are as much as 2cm away from the bill tip.

Touch feeding confers several advantages upon its practitioners. For one thing, they don't need to spread out widely over the mud surface in order to forage. Sight-feeders, by contrast, always require a degree of privacy to work, because a neighbour coming too near might spook surface prey or distract the hunter. Touch feeding can thus be done in large, tight-knit groups without

Knots hunch down to plough the surface of the mud.

When waders bunch together to feed, as these Sanderlings are doing, you can be sure they are feeding by touch.

fear of intrusion, allowing a higher density of birds to partake.

One another advantage is that touch feeding can be done at any time of day or night. Sight feeding, by contrast, is a daylight activity by its very nature: a blanket of darkness over the mud denies the birds their optimum feeding conditions – although a few may use the light of a full moon. In theory at least, such problems should not dog touch-feeders, since they are not using their eyes.

One snag, though, is that tactile foraging is a very popular pursuit. The mud can be a little crowded at times, and many birds may have to indulge in second-hand foraging, going over well-trodden ground, especially where the ooze is thin and gentle to probing bills. This

sort of situation can create intense competition among birds, not only among their own kind but between different species as well. It's a story that repeats itself wherever food is abundant to wild birds: there are almost inevitably too many takers.

But the waders, at least, have got round this problem by finding a subtle way to divide the spoils. For, despite the apparent homogeneity of the intertidal habitat, each species has its own specialised way of looting it – just as in the human world every company has its own ploy for selling, let's say, car insurance. Thus, the intertidal birds differ between themselves in three main ways: in

the depth to which they probe; in the depth of water in which they work; and in the refinements to their foraging technique. (And, funnily enough, insurance salesmen often probe the depths, too).

You don't need to watch birds in the act of feeding to get an idea of how deep they probe: the bill tells you. The Bar-tailed Godwit's, for example, is up to 10cm long, which enables it to reach a community of organisms that lie beyond the reach of, say, a Dunlin, whose bill is only 4cm long. This means that lugworms, whose burrows may reach down 15cm into the mud, are on the menu for godwits but not – in theory, at least – Dunlins. Each mud-probing wader has a bill of slightly different length. The Curlew has the longest, followed by the two godwits, then the Oystercatcher, Redshank, Dunlin and, finally, the Knot. Each can only probe as far as its bill will take it, and its diet is determined accordingly.

And although all these birds are called waders, not all of them actually like to get their feet wet. Dunlins, Knots and Oystercatchers, for example, all have relatively short legs, and don't wade in very far, if at all. Neither, surprisingly, does the distinctly leggy Curlew, despite towering over all the rest when standing. The waders that really earn the label are the godwits. These birds typically feed in the water itself, where the mud is softest and they find it easy to probe in their long, largely straight bills. When probing, godwits have the very distinctive habit of immersing their head in the water, presumably closing their eyes and completely surrendering to touch. Greenshanks, when they visit our estuaries on migration, are also good paddlers. Working up to their bellies, they often run along in the water chasing small fish. Avocets, found in a few of our estuaries, wade so deep that they often find themselves swimming.

The final difference between these touch-feeders lies in their specific feeding techniques. Here the distinctions between species become more subtle. For example, the Dunlin and Knot feed over the same mud, and their bills are of comparable length. The Knot's bill, however, is slightly thicker, enabling it to practise to advantage a technique called "ploughing", in which the bird immerses its bill into very soft mud and then moves forward, as though ploughing a furrow, looking a bit like a dog nosing in the litter. The Dunlin, with its thinner and slightly curved bill, rarely does this. Instead, if a Dunlin comes upon an area with a particularly high density of food, it will probe several times into the mud in quick succession, only just lifting its bill out each time. Were it to make an impact in the substrate, this technique would leave several holes very close together.

It is known as "stitching", which neatly describes the sewing-like action, and is also practised by godwits in the shallows and by Snipe on freshwater marshes.

Arctic exodus

Despite the year-round abundance of food on offer, the gathering of birds on estuaries is very much a seasonal phenomenon. Once March approaches, the first waders and gulls start heading off for their breeding grounds. The Brent Geese, too, who have spent the winter gorging themselves on eel-grass growing near the low water-line, depart on a long journey that will take them, step by step, into the depths of the Arctic. Later on, in April and May, many of the waders will also make their final dash for these remote latitudes, where their breeding season in the superabundant tundra will be short and wild. Each species has its own destination: Knots go to Greenland; godwits to Iceland and Russia; Grey Plovers to Siberia; and Sanderlings almost to the edge of the High Arctic pack ice. The birds that we see on temperate mudflats are soon crossing paths with Arctic Foxes and perhaps even Polar Bears, and they switch to a diet of insects on the mosquito-infested pools, forsaking their estuarine skills. Many assume fine plumage, with red and chestnut and bold patches of black, making a dramatic transformation in appearance as well as lifestyle. For a few months, they truly leave us behind.

A few birds do remain, but the problem is that the estuary is not really a suitable place for breeding. The ebb and flow of the tide, such a boon for mixing the mud and serving bulk food in the off-season, becomes a liability, its periodic inundations a threat to nests or very young chicks. So those few species that do breed tend to cling to the margins: Redshanks and Black-headed Gulls choose the salt marsh, flirting with high water, especially at spring tides; Shelducks prefer the nearby sand dunes; and Ringed Plovers and terns hide away in the dry shingle. For a while the inhabitants find it hard to cope with the estuary's fickle nature. In the breeding season the crowds have gone and the place seems unusually quiet.

Thus, in summer, the estuary's bird populations reach their lowest point. In July the first returnees from the Arctic trickle back, augmented by others, then still others, in August and September. Once October begins the estuary begins to fill up again, to become its crowded self by the middle of the winter. The comings and goings of birds mirror the tidal ebb and flow on this most capricious of habitats.

An Oystercatcher about to wield its axe.

Oystercatchers as tradesmen

WADERS FEEDING on the mud appear almost casually efficient. They extract shellfish and other items without much fuss or flourish, and it is easy to imagine that, should you suddenly wake up one morning transformed into an Oystercatcher, say, you would simply settle into an easy rhythm and feed away to your heart's content. But you'd be wrong: feeding on shellfish is not easy at all. The prey is awkward and intransigent, and often well hidden. It does, after all, want to avoid being eaten. So waders on the mud are better seen as skilled professionals – as clever, for example, as those snooker players that make fiendishly difficult potting seem so ridiculously easy. If you try playing snooker or extracting shellfish for a living without a great deal of practice, you'll end up the same way: hungry.

Shellfish extraction, therefore, should be looked upon as an art – or, perhaps to be more accurate, a trade. It is, after all, how these birds make their day-to-day living. And just as different people enter different trades, so it is possible for different individuals of the same species, notably Oystercatchers, to pursue different lines of work. There is, perhaps surprisingly, more than one way to open an obdurate mollusc.

Oystercatchers ply their trade in two different ways: there are the Hammerers and the Stabbers. Despite sounding like violent street gangs, these are effectively tradesmen's guilds, with a membership and even a physical identity. The casual birdwatcher can quickly tell to which group each bird belongs.

The Hammerers go about their business in a rather crude fashion, and it is tempting to consider them as the labourers among Oystercatchers. Having extracted cockles from the mud or ripped mussels from their beds, the Hammerers lodge them on the substrate and smash them open with a number of well aimed blows. Although their hits may look random, they are actually aimed close to the adductor muscle, the one that holds the two shells of a bivalve tightly shut. Once the adductor is unveiled and cut, all the bivalve's resistance is futile and the Oystercatcher can clean the mollusc out of its shell with ease.

The Stabbers, by contrast, are the artisans. They also target the adductor muscle, but instead of smashing the mollusc's shell they use surgical precision to prise their bill tip in between the two valves and feel their way to the adductor, which they then snip open. Once again the valves fall apart like the pages of a book and the Oystercatcher can eat the flesh. On occasion, the birds even creep up on an unsuspecting mollusc and slit the adductor before the shellfish has a chance to shut its valves.

These very different skills, stabbing and hammering, exploit different characteristics of the Oystercatcher's bill. Although it looks long and substantial, the bill is actually narrow if viewed from above or below – or, to use the correct term, "laterally flattened", a little like a letter opener. So Stabbers can use it as a fine instrument to slice their way in between the valves. But despite being narrow it is also extremely tough. The bill actually consists of two parts, an inner bony core and a strong outer protective sheath, the latter hardest towards the tip. So it is in no danger of being broken when used as a blunt, bludgeoning instrument by a Hammerer.

Nonetheless, the continual act of hammering does have an effect on the bill's shape, blunting the tip and thickening the central region to make the whole thing look a little like a chisel. The Stabber's bill, on the other hand, is more even in shape, with a sharper point – which also makes it suitable for touch feeding, since a sharp bill slips more easily into the mud than a blunt one. So the birder wishing to distinguish between the two should start by looking at Oystercatchers on the mud and then check out those feeding on rocks or mussel beds. With practice, the differences become quite easy to detect.

But, you might ask, what makes an Oystercatcher a member of one trade union or another? Is a bird confined to its station for life? The answer to the first question lies not with nature, but with nurture. Young Oystercatchers take a great deal of time learning how to feed, and they do so by watching their parents. They are unique among young birds in that despite hatching in a well-developed, fluffy and peripatetic state, they are unable to feed themselves. They are raring to go, but their prey is just too difficult to get hold of. So instead, like tradesmen and tradeswomen of old, they watch and learn, effectively serving an apprenticeship. Meanwhile they are fed by their parents. It will be some weeks before they become fully independent, and many do not make it through their difficult training period.

And once an oystercatcher has learnt its parents' trade, there is no reason why it should not pick up the other technique, too. An individual, it seems, can shift from Hammerer to Stabber when the need arises, if only on a temporary basis. Nonetheless, it seems likely that most birds are inherently better at one task than another, and that these aptitudes may well pass down the family line. If there is a genetic link, perhaps one day the two trades will diverge, and Stabbers, for example, will only pair with Stabbers, until they become a separate species? We cannot yet tell whether this will happen, but it is an intriguing possibility.

A bit of stealth is needed for Stabbers.

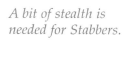

With this fish...

EACH SUMMER Terns arrive in our coastal waters and add a dash of elegance to our roll-call of seabirds. They are a bit like gulls to look at, but they are far more graceful and angular, with sharp corners everywhere – sharp bills, sharp tails and sharp wing-tips. They also have sharp calls. Terns were once called sea swallows, and they live up to this description well, with their long, forked tails and sweeping flight. Like Swallows they are summer migrants, arriving and departing at the same time as their land-based counterparts.

Terns are sociable and noisy. They are like those under-confident people who always set their voice at a slightly higher volume than the rest. Their colonies on shingle banks and islands produce a constant chorus of squeals and screams, ensuring that the neighbours never get a moment's peace. And as well as assaulting eardrums everywhere, terns are also the bane of the local fish population. Their long bills are typical of those of fish-eaters, sharp and dagger-like for knifing through the water, and their highly modified, long, pointed wings enable them to hover over the water before plunging in after whatever they have seen. Terns certainly hunt in style. They are like maritime kestrels, holding position in the air before a theatrical splash and grab.

Catching fish is a skill that is dependent upon weather conditions. Terns prefer a moderate wind and some waves to no wind at all, though a very strong blow may force them to seek more sheltered waters for their fishing. Some terns also prefer to hunt on a rising tide, especially around estuaries. And fish are unpredictable creatures, massing at different places at different times, so the terns must always be alert to an opportunity. All these variables make fishing quite a meritocratic activity, with some birds clearly much more skilled than others, and able to feed themselves somewhat more comfortably. But, in a sense, every single catch is a small triumph.

The very difficulty of fishing explains why, in the courtship language of the Common Tern, the presentation of a freshly caught fish is a sensuous, almost erotic signal between one bird and another. It carries with it profound implications of provision, competence and fertility that every bird understands. Thus almost every nuptial display of the Common Tern involves the carrying of a fish, and even the delicate moments prior to copulation may be eased by the giving and receiving of this fresh, scaly gift. It is a practical, as well as an amorous way of expressing a fondness and togetherness.

Right at the beginning of the season, a young Common Tern setting out on its quest to breed needs to master this language straight away. Young males advertise their presence with a highly public ritual known as a "low flight". This is the Common Tern equivalent of cruising through the neighbourhood in a fancy car. Having caught a fish, the bird returns to the colony and flies very slowly over the assembled birds, with heavy wing-beats and calling even more loudly than usual. It makes several passes a few feet above ground, and its message is unambiguous to all: 'Look at me: I can catch and provide'. The older, experienced birds, no doubt, just roll their eyes and grumble about the noise.

Catching fish is a highly prized skill among terns.

If the display elicits interest, either in the form of inciting a rival male or attracting a female, a "high flight" may ensue, with two or three birds taking part. This skittish display lives up to its name; the birds' light wing-beats take them up in a spiral and they may not level out until they reach a height of 200m or more, still visible and audible from the ground. Up here the birds' qualities are less obvious to their potential partners below, so they make alternating fly-pasts in

private, one simply going in front of the other and then dropping back, the passing bird maintaining a posture with its head bent down and tail lifted up. The male usually holds on to its fish as it flies past, to ensure that its message is clear – even at these lofty heights.

It is now that the more serious part of courtship starts. As soon as two Common Terns have paired off, the male falls into the role of provider. Instead of showing off with a fish, and being loud and brash, he now quietly goes about bringing his female regular meals, about six per day, one fish per serving. Without any ceremony, he slips off periodically to the fishing grounds to ensure that both he and his mate are fed adequately. The extent of his provision is vital. With the birds freshly paired, their partnership still hangs in the balance; they have entered a honeymoon period, a time when things can still go wrong. The female's first taste of being a "kept woman" will give her a good idea of her mate's competence as a provider for the chicks. She can still ditch him if his efforts somehow fall short.

These efforts on the part of the male allow the female to get into condition for breeding without the burden of having to find her own food. Most importantly, she must get through the phase of forming the three or so eggs inside her, a process that requires much the same heavy expenditure of energy as any pregnancy. Later on, she will also be the main incubator, taking on about three-quarters of this duty, which also consumes a lot of energy. So the hunting trips of the male are in deadly earnest: unproductive fishing expeditions during this phase may result in smaller eggs and weaker young, if indeed the young hatch at all.

Thus, a tern colony in summer becomes a place of fish-passing ceremonies, and remains so until the very end of the breeding season. At first it is the females that bow before the arriving males, calling in plaintive fashion and opening their bills for food. Later on, of course, the youngsters will do just the same. They will beg until after fledging, and some young terns may even leave with their parents on the first leg of their southward migratory journey, pleading for food as they go.

Thus the Common Tern colony departs in the same way that it arrived: with shrieks, splashes and fishy gifts.

It's all because the lady loves…

The Shelduck's summer festival

ALL BIRDS change their feathers at least once a year. For most, the annual moult is a bit of a pain: it saps their energy and makes them vulnerable to predation, robbing them of some of their natural ebullience and confining them to the bowels of bushes. But for a few birds, the moult is much less of an ordeal. In fact, more than anything, it seems to be an excuse for an almighty knees-up.

No species in Britain handles its moulting season with such aplomb as the Shelduck, a black, white and chestnut duck with a long neck and a splendid waxy red bill that is forever poking into estuarine goo. In common with many waterfowl, the Shelduck is an impetuous shedder of feathers, letting as many go as possible in the shortest time in order to get the whole thing over. In its haste it sheds so many flight feathers simultaneously that, for a while, it cannot take off at all, but merely swims forlornly about.

The Shelduck's breakneck approach to moulting puts it in extreme peril from predators. After all, ducks are good to eat, and flightless ones are pure temptation. What it must do, therefore, is to avoid being – pardon the pun – a sitting duck. That means heading off before the moult begins and finding somewhere else to drop its feathers, somewhere with fewer predators but plenty of food. So the Shelducks do exactly that, embarking on a special interest package tour, officially known as a moult migration.

Their flight takes them across the North Sea to a paradise – at least in Shelduck terms – of mudflats off northern Germany called the Grosser Knechtsand. Something equivalent to a Shelduck health farm, it is a massive estuary and area of shallow sea extending many miles out from the coast, well out of reach of most predators. It is also superabundantly rich in all the food that Shelducks like. In short, it is the perfect moulting spot.

The moult migration begins in mid-June when, on a fine night with a kind westerly wind, the adolescent Shelducks, still too young to breed, take off into the darkness. Ducks are powerful fliers and it is almost certain that they make the journey in a single flight, arriving at their destination some time the following morning. Adults that have failed to breed set off almost immediately afterward; they have no need to linger and can find consolation for their failure in the excitable moulting-ground atmosphere. By July it is it the turn of the breeding birds to depart, and by month's end all but a few of the Shelducks in the whole of Western Europe are concentrated in the forgiving waters of the Grosser Knechtsand.

The sheer number of birds involved is remarkable. Up to 200,000 tricoloured ducks may gather along less than eighty kilometres of German coast, creating a pattern of well spaced bright spots on the murky mud. Participants in this moult-fest come from as far away as Southern France, Ireland and Scandinavia, all pulled in by the superb conditions. And although many waterfowl perform moult migrations, it is the high

A bunch of delegates on the Waddenzee.

brood in a nursery with dozens of other chicks, under the supervision of small numbers of "crèche-guards". The guards may be successful parents or even failed breeders who, in a way not yet understood, are enlisted to look after that year's hatchlings. The minders don't do very much, but they can at least give alarm calls and be a reassuring presence to their charges, which may number up to a hundred. And, importantly, they don't just fly off when their turn to moult comes round. Instead, driven by a sense of responsibility, they undertake their own feather makeover on-site, missing all the year's fun at the Shelducks' summer festival. They and the chicks make for rather a sorry sight, abandoned by the rest of the population. Britain is almost empty of Shelducks in the late summer.

And they are certainly missing something. The vast concentration of birds in the Grosser Knechtsand must be highly stimulating to all the arriving Shelducks, and an ample food supply is always a boon to any bird anywhere. One suspects that, if there wasn't the distraction of having to breed, a good many Shelducks would choose to remain in this part of the North Sea for the rest of their lives. They are certainly in no hurry to return after the moult. Like a human being that starts to rather enjoy sick leave, the Shelducks find every excuse to delay their return to "normal" life, often tarrying until October or even later before starting their journey back, many weeks after their moult is complete. Some individuals do not return again to their breeding sites until January.

The Shelduck, therefore, has transformed what is a tiresome chore for most birds into the highlight of its year.

A happy family scene? No, these are abandoned juvenile Shelducks with their crèche-guards.

percentage of population gathered in just one locality that makes the Shelduck's version unique. If you're a Shelduck, there's only one place to be.

Well actually, this isn't quite true. Another curiosity about Shelduck moult migration is the timing: it clashes with the end of the breeding season. This means that the adult Shelducks depart on their jolly before the ducklings are fully independent, leaving the latter to fend for themselves while the parents fly off abroad to indulge. The strategy recalls those infamous cases of human parents who jet off and leave their offspring "home alone" then find themselves in court when they return from holiday.

In fact, the strategy is not as callous as it first appears. Before the adults leave, they deposit their

Curves and ways

A CURLEW'S bill is such an obvious and integral part of its body that it seems rather rude to question its purpose. After all, if we met someone with an extraordinarily long nose, we would probably talk about anything to them except what was most clearly before our eyes. But, in the natural world, pretty much everything has a function, and often the more eyebrow-raising it is, the more precisely it fits in somewhere. The Curlew's bill is the perfect example.

This remarkable appendage is both very long and deliciously downwardly curved. The length is easy enough to understand: it enables the Curlew to probe more deeply than other waders, so that, should the shorter-billed birds be taking all the food near the surface, the Curlew can work deeper down. But what about the curve? What use is that?

If you've recently had a dental appointment, you will probably recall with requisite horror the first part of your check-up – that moment when the dentist takes an instrument to poke around and probe the cracks in your teeth. This instrument, you might have noticed, has a curved tip, and although it does not really resemble the Curlew's bill, some of the working principles are the same.

Your mouth is an entrance. Moreover, the inside of your mouth is wider than the circle made by your lips. Similar mouths occur in all sorts of places, including the small crevices in which crabs and other tasty invertebrates hide on the shore. When a Curlew is investigating these mini-caves with its bill, the curve allows it to work more effectively in the lobby of the burrow, so to speak, and to grab hold of whatever lurks inside. In theory, the curvature also gives the tip of the bill a wider turning circle than a straight bill would allow, so that a bird that has inserted its beak into the gooey mud can turn it around while still immersed and make use of a wide subterranean reach.

Scientists tell us that a curved bill also makes it easier for this long-legged bird to reach and process food on the surface. So, overall, it would seem that the design is perfect and the bill indispensable.

The Curlew's long, curved bill enables it to deal with tricky customers.

Which raises the question: why don't all waders have curved bills?

Well, like everything, the shape has an inherent snag. The curvature makes the bill inherently weaker than a straight bill would be, leaving it more vulnerable to damage in the normal course of wear and tear. So, in order to prevent bills snapping every time Curlews go feeding, the structure is fitted with internal struts and is specially thickened to guard against this hazard. And this arrangement means, unfortunately, that in the part of the bill furthest from the mouth, with all the internal scaffolding, there is no room for the tongue when the bill is shut.

This is a bit awkward. Most waders have tongues equivalent to the length of their bill, which they use to get a quick purchase on food acquired at the tip. Curlews cannot do this. Instead, they must pull larger items out of the mud completely when feeding and juggle them slightly before swallowing. This must be somewhat inconvenient, and also allows a chance for the food to fall out or escape. So the Curlew's bill is not a perfect tool. Nonetheless, it works well enough for its owner to find an exclusive niche among the many waders working an estuary.

SEA CLIFFS

The high life

IF THERE is one bird habitat that could be compared to a city, it is the sea cliff, with its high-rise structure, close living conditions, constant noise, bustle, piles of waste, and smell. It would be an unusual city, though. For at least a third of the year it is almost deserted as many of its inhabitants evacuate to the surrounding sea, leaving behind empty ledges and groups of bored-looking gulls.

A GOOD many of the birds of the sea cliff, you see, are here by default. They are not cliff-dwellers at all, but really seabirds that use this half-land habitat as a temporary breeding base. You might almost compare them to owners of holiday cottages: if you live in London but spend a few weeks every summer at your property in Wales, that does not make you Welsh, just as renting a cliff or offshore island for a few weeks in summer doesn't make you a cliff bird. Most of us have an image of a cliff-nesting seabird, such as a Puffin, waddling over thrift-covered rocks close to its burrow. Yet the Puffin arrives offshore in March, doesn't settle on a burrow until April and has left for good before the end of August. For the rest of the year it reveals its true self as it swims in the deep waters of the Atlantic and dives for fish. It is not adapted to land at all; it is adapted to the sea.

If the birds of the sea cliffs are such fleeting inhabitants, why, then, do they come here at all? The answer, put simply, is that you cannot make a nest on the sea; you have to find some dry land. And despite the fact that a few seabirds commute some distance inland to breed, for the majority the border between land and sea presents their best option. It's rather like living close to your workplace. Very few occupants ever find food, for themselves or their young, on the cliff itself. They will have to make continual trips out to sea, so they might as well base themselves as close to it as possible.

In this respect, cliffs have certain advantages over other coastal habitats. Those seabirds that

Previous spread: A busy cliff-top panorama, with Puffins (foreground), Great Black-backed Gull (right), Herring Gulls (left), Kittiwakes and Guillemots (background).

Below: There's not much privacy in a Gannet colony…

choose this precipitous habitat for their nest sites find that cliffs, especially those towering, slippery ones at whose base the waves are constantly pounding, make unusually safe places. A predatory land mammal such as a fox or rat would be foolish indeed to risk its neck trying to find food atop these natural skyscrapers, so the birds are safe from all of these. Sea cliffs on offshore islets are best, since many of these have no land predators at all, not even on the cliff-top turf.

Going colonial

One of the strongest images of the sea cliff in Britain is of rock-faces teeming with birds. We hear statistics from those who somehow manage to count these masses: 67,000 Kittiwakes, 15,000 Puffins, 1000 Razorbills and so on. In our wide-eyed wonder we can easily fail to ask the obvious question: why do all these birds nest so close together? Aren't there enough cliff-tops to enable them all to spread out?

The answer, simply put, is no. The chances are that some seabirds would probably prefer to nest well apart from the rest if they could: Fulmars, for example, are rather bad neighbours, and Great Black-backed Gulls are murderous neighbours from Hell, which often find their own separate spot anyway. For the majority, however, there is simply not enough room to have that luxury, and so they nest in crowded colonies, with all the noise and hassle.

Colonial nesting does have its benefits, though. For example, a group of Gannets makes a pretty formidable deterrent to a flying nest-predator, such as a gull or skua, and certainly a more effective one than a single defender on its own. Gulls themselves are also highly aggressive in communal defence, and almost any large gathering of birds can make an unsettling rumpus if needed. So colonies as a whole do offer some safety in numbers. Colonies can also be very stimulating places, and there is some evidence that the sight of lots of neighbours displaying, copulating and feeding young can help birds get physiologically primed for their breeding duties – just as baby production among groups of human friends can engender broodiness in even the most unlikely suspects.

It has also been suggested that colonial living may indirectly help birds feed their young. Since these cliff dwellers commute out to sea, birds on an outward journey in search of provision can easily observe their colleagues returning and thus, in theory, are led to fruitful waters. Although such

...but Shags hide away in sheltered corners, including sea-caves.

an idea is difficult to prove, it is hard to imagine any bird ignoring such information and simply going its own way.

Living on the ledge

The taller cliffs and islands along the British coast, those formed of tough rocks such as granite, limestone and sandstone that are not easily eroded by the action of waves, wind and rain, often provide breeding sites for quite a number of species at the same time. This means that, rather than hosting one colony of a single species, many cliffs support several different overlapping colonies. Cliffs are never uniform in structure, and different parts of the same cliff suit different species. For example, most Shags nest at the bottom of the cliff and most Fulmars at the top, while birds such as Kittiwakes and Guillemots fill the space in the middle. Some birds select the turf that crowns the cliff, and still others prefer irregular features such as sea-caves or coves. So each species finds its niche; even on a

casual visit it's easy to observe this separation and stratification.

Kittiwakes occupy the most vertical sections of the cliff. These are inoffensive members of the gull family that feed on fish rather than scrapping at rubbish dumps or raiding the nests of other birds, as some of their cousins are wont to do. They are as noisy as other Gulls, however, and whole cliffs can be dominated by their slightly bugling wails, which are said to have given rise to their name. These birds can build a nest on the slightest of projections, affixing them to the rock using a combination of their own guano and stocky green seaweed. They then add mud, grass and moss, if available, and tread down every new item of material in order to compact the nest. Eventually a cup is formed at the top, and the young Kittiwakes are born into the most precarious nest site in Britain. The chicks of most Gulls are peripatetic when young, wandering around their parents' mini-territory, but Kittiwake chicks – sensibly enough – remain very much stationary on the nest.

Stand and deliver – a Kittiwake about to regurgitate food for its chick.

Where the cliff structure offers ledges, Guillemots can also find a place. These birds – which, like Puffins, are members of the Auk family – lay a single egg, and their territory allows just enough room for one bird to stand by the egg while its partner perches nearby. This territory is, in fact, the smallest of any bird in the world. Guillemots on eggs commonly incubate whilst in physical contact with their neighbours along the ledge, and sometimes with several other birds. Furthermore, they can occupy such narrow ledges that they have no protection from the wind or rain. It must be pretty uncomfortable.

Guillemot eggs have a couple of interesting adaptations to the crowded cliff-ledge. They are quite large eggs and have a distinct pear-shape, which means that, should they receive an accidental knock from a parent or neighbour, they

will roll in a circle rather than off the cliff (although some, inevitably, tumble to their doom). Also, every Guillemot egg also has its own unique, recognisable pattern of spots and squiggles, giving the adults a good chance of making sure they find and incubate the right egg among the massed ranks of the colony.

A close relative of the Guillemot, the Razorbill, occupies the broader ledges of the mid-cliff, and collects into smaller colonies. These birds do not live shoulder to shoulder, and their housing is undoubtedly of a more comfortable style than that of their relatives, giving them some room to breathe. Some Razorbills, indeed, have a roof over their head in the form of an overhang, which is a rare luxury indeed. Interestingly, Razorbill eggs are more rounded in shape than those of Guillemots, since the greater width of their ledges means that the chance rolling of an egg need not necessarily be a catastrophe.

Feel the width

The birdlife of the less vertical parts of the cliff face tends to be determined by how broad the ledges and other features are. Fulmars need a little more room than Razorbills, Shags more than Fulmars, Cormorants more than Shags, and Gannets need the broadest surface of all. Gannets are so large that their sites must also have a lot of draught to help them spread their wings and let the wind whisk them off their breeding rocks. Many Gannet colonies are sited at the top of sea-stacks and islands, simply to allow these big birds easy access. If a Gannet gets its approach to the nest site wrong, it will find itself stabbed by the bills of angry neighbours, but with the wind to help it make a precision landing, this can usually be avoided.

Towards the bottom of many cliffs, where the unrelenting battering of the waves eats into the hardest of rocks, a micro-habitat of caverns and large boulders can form, home to a characteristic suite of birds that may nest above the level of the spray. This includes the Shag, which prefers much more sheltered sites than its relative the Cormorant, and will often place its nest up against or even under a rock. Also, on occasions Puffins and Storm Petrels will use crevices and fissures down here. But the most typical bird of such places, particularly the boulder screes, and one that chooses this over all other niches offered by cliffs, is the Black Guillemot. This is one of our scarcer sea cliff dwellers, and also one of the few that often forsakes colonial nesting in favour of holding a discrete territory; indeed, even colonies of this bird are well spaced and modest in size, a far cry from the usual multitudes.

There is another characteristic of the Black Guillemot that is unusual among members of its family: it often lays two eggs instead of one. The reason for this seems to be that Black Guillemots find it easier to provide for their young than do the others. These dark-clad Auks are primarily inshore feeders, specialising on scouring the seabed itself, rather than open water. They rarely travel further than 4km on a commuting trip, and thus by feeding close at hand they cut down the time and effort they must expend on seeking food for their progeny. Guillemots, Razorbills and Puffins, on the other hand, often have to commute tens of kilometres to obtain the free-swimming fish that they need. These birds rarely come to the nest more than six times a day, whereas the Black Guillemot may come as often as fifteen times. Nevertheless, inshore feeding also keeps Black Guillemot numbers low; if these Auks nested at the density of the rest, their local supplies of food would quickly run out.

The high tops

Just as the lower parts of the cliff have specialised tenants, so do the upper reaches, where the bare rock gives way to turf. This is often the best site for Fulmars and Puffins, the former using wide ledges and the latter making burrows in the soil. Where disturbance is minimal and ground predators are excluded, which is usually on islands, such birds as Manx Shearwaters and Storm and Leach's Petrels will also nest on the top of the cliffs, using rabbit holes and crevices in walls and buildings. All these species travel well out to sea to find food for their young, and the Shearwaters and Petrels only visit their burrows at night. All of them make loud cackling and cat-erwauling sounds, which are the very essence of offshore islands in the short darkness of summer.

Most of the cliff-living Gulls also nest near the top, where they require a little horizontal space to allow their youngsters to run around. Most of these birds will be Herring Gulls, but many cliffs are also home to Lesser Black-backed and Great Black-backed Gulls. These large, powerful birds can be real pests to other seabirds, snatching eggs and chicks. The largest species, the Great Black-backed, will even eat the adults of smaller birds such as Puffins. Gulls will also steal food that smaller birds are bringing back to feed their young. Their pres-ence, and that of the menacing skuas nesting on nearby moorland, means that every seabird has to keep a constant lookout for danger and trouble.

'Next time you get it' – a Fulmar threatens to spew out stomach oil.

Fulmars, for their part, have a novel deterrent against these unwelcome intruders. Should any uninvited predator come within range, they will disgorge their stomach oil upon it. In fact, they will spit it out with deadly accuracy. The smelly, gooey oil does no good at all to a bird's plumage, compromising its waterproofing. Thus this behaviour is a highly effective defence measure, allowing Fulmars to occupy their nests out in the open by both day and night. When Fulmar eggs hatch, the adults take turns to guard their chick for about 14 days; after this their offspring is capable of spitting out its own stomach oil and taking care of itself.

Not all the predators of the cliff are seabirds themselves – at least not in the traditional sense of the word. Some sea cliffs in Northern and Western Scotland are occupied by the thrillingly dangerous White-tailed Eagle, a huge predator that will happily snatch other birds from the water. Golden Eagles may also patrol seabird colonies, and Peregrines customarily do.

The Peregrines, however, are more interested in catching pigeons. These land birds also use sea cliffs as a habitat, and are often very common, flying about in their usual dolly-mixture flocks of different colours. The pigeon that most of us recognise, and the one that ornithologists tend to call the Feral Pigeon, is in fact as much a bird of the cliffs as any of the seabirds mentioned above. Long before people ever noticed pigeons and used them for food or homing, the ancestor of them all lived on cliffs in places like these. Their direct descendants, those that retain ancestral plumage, are officially called Rock Doves. They nest, much as the seabirds do, in clefts and on ledges.

No human city is complete without its pigeons, so perhaps their existence on sea cliffs confirms the metropolitan nature of this habitat. Sea cliffs – at least to a seabird – are cities just like any other.

Gulls aloud!

Confidence – the Herring Gull's Long Call.

HAVE YOU ever had difficulty telling a male Herring Gull from a female? Well, here's some news for you: so do the gulls themselves. The plumage of the sexes is identical, and as a result it can be very difficult, in the scrimmage of a cliff-top colony, for a gull to recognise neighbour, foe or significant other with speed and certainty. As a result a Herring Gull colony in spring is a place of gesture and nuance, ritual and ceremony, where the birds communicate with movements and signals, a bit like a convention of Freemasons. Only by adopting the appropriate sign language, together with an accompanying call, can the members of a colony sort themselves into pairs and territories, and live in understanding and peace.

If you visit the colony early in the season, it rings with noisy calls, as territory holders proclaim to one and all that they are in residence. This proclamatory "long call" is usually made by male birds, and it consists of an extended series of loud yells which begin slowly and then speed up; it's a very familiar sound of the seaside. While belting it out, the birds stand still and at first bow their heads at the beginning of the phrase so that they are looking at their feet, but then raise their bill to the heavens as they get into their stride – just like an opera singer raising hands to the heavens to enhance the power of a long note. Long calls are very loud, and they are often the bane of existence for residents of coastal towns where the gulls nest on the rooftops.

Once a male gull has established his presence, deafening everyone in the process, he will inevitably be visited by females. These visitors are of two kinds: "soliciting" females, who are simply turning up for a preliminary meeting equivalent to a first date; and "currently resident" females, who are staying around for a while to get to know the male and are, in human terms, effectively the current girlfriend – though, like any girlfriend, their chances of actually staying the course are by no means guaranteed. When females land on a territory they almost always assume what is known as a "hunched" posture, making themselves look rather small and keeping their head down at shoulder-level. Although to our eyes they might look a bit fed up, what they are offering is appeasement, reducing the male's

Courtship – a Herring Gull about to throw up an offering.

natural aggression. Once they have been accepted, they will soon begin to make begging gestures towards the male, nodding their heads and shaping to peck his bill. It looks annoying to us, and most males seem highly reluctant to be drawn into giving the female what she is requesting, regurgitated food. Many, indeed, tease their females by coughing up some morsel into the bill only to swallow it again. But eventually, presumably because of a female's persistence or attractiveness, a male gull will regurgitate his latest meal on to the ground as an offering to his potential mate.

It seems revolting to us. Imagine if a man took his date out to dinner and, rather than ordering food, actually puked up in front of her; she wouldn't be very impressed! To a female gull, however, such a gesture is a first move towards intimacy, and gulls so provided are well on the way to be paired off. The offerings of food, which increase as the pair bond strengthens, help the female get into condition for laying eggs. The ritual of begging and providing soon becomes routine.

Every so often, of course, a male gull will have its territorial borders invaded by a rival. This doesn't only happen at the beginning of the season when territorial boundaries are still quite fluid, but also whenever an unpaired bird feels obliged to force its way between territories in a desperate effort to salvage something from its breeding season. Either way, a male must always be on the alert for unwelcome trespassing.

A stand-off between two rival gulls is fraught with tension, and the stakes are very high: it can, after all, determine breeding success for the whole season. At first the territory holder seems to be frozen on the spot, standing still and facing straight ahead with eyes wide open. In fact, this gesture, known as the "alert upright posture", can be intimidating enough to frighten away intruders on its own. But more often the two birds quickly assume the "aggressive upright posture", facing each other with head held high and bill pointing down, their wings drooped slightly – like two cowboys ready to draw. They then usually approach each other with stiff, cautious footsteps, and will sometimes even charge.

Anger – a Herring Gull "Grass-pulling".

Sometimes the two feuding birds give the appearance of being quite unable to know what to do, and when this happens they will vent their aggression upon nearby objects, such as grass or lumps of earth. Opening up their wings, they will suddenly grab the offending object and pull at it – a statement of frustration equivalent to our kicking the cat. In some cases this, too, can precipitate a retreat. More often, though, the aggression just boils over and the birds fight, tugging and pecking at each other. Most disputes are resolved very quickly in this way.

On occasion a male and female Herring Gull find themselves threatened on their territory as a pair. When this happens they frequently adopt a rather odd display known as "choking". Making quiet chuckling calls, each bird flexes its legs, leans over and points its bill to the ground, as if it were about to throw up into a sink. Instead it simply moves its head up and down in a retching movement and continues to call. At times, male and female may perform the "choking" ceremony in the absence of rivals, and evidently for their own benefit.

With so many ways of getting their message across, one would imagine that Herring Gulls rarely, if ever, get their wires crossed. Nevertheless, there is one highly unusual phenomenon that might suggest otherwise: the regular formation of female-female pairs. Whether these occur by mistake, or whether females sometimes resort to homosexual partnerships in the absence of enough males is not known for sure, but there are definitely occasions when two females look after a brood of eggs that are presumably fertilised by male neighbours.

That raises some interesting questions. How, for example, does the gesturing then work, and how do the females solicit enough attention from nearby males to be inseminated, yet still manage to remain paired to another female? Maybe, as yet, we still have a lot to learn about the language of Herring Gulls.

Passion – two Herring Gulls about to mate.

The hard-working Puffin

IN MANY ways, it must be good to be a seabird. In life expectancy, for example, you have a distinct advantage over your terrestrial equivalents. On land, a bird the size of a Puffin, such as a pigeon, would be fortunate to live for more than five years; but a Puffin itself has much better prospects, with the average individual passing ten years, and a few even reaching the grand old age of 30. And for all that time a Puffin need only think about finding enough fish to keep its belly full; a survival rate of 95% of adults every year suggests that this cannot be too difficult.

Nevertheless, in one respect the life of a seabird is harder than most: this is the sheer effort it must expend every breeding season just to bring its egg to independent chick-hood. We are regularly told that a Great Tit, for example, has to make 500 visits a day to keep its brood fed, which is pretty impressive. But that's only for only 18 days at the most, whereas the Puffin has to feed its voracious chick for up to 44 days. And that is by no means its only burden.

Early in the year it is tempting to think that Puffins are reluctant to begin their exhausting breeding schedule. Flocks hang about in the sea, loafing beside their cliffs or islands, as though putting things off. Sometimes they come in to land at last, only to evacuate en masse for the slightest of reasons – even a change in the weather. Though the first birds turn up on site as early as March, breeding rarely gets underway before May. But the Puffins are biding their time, feeding up and getting slowly into condition for the twelve-week marathon of toil and endeavour that lies ahead.

The first challenge is finding a place to breed. For most seabirds this is easy, since pairs can simply select their ledge or crevice from a whole range of options. But for Puffins things are more difficult. These birds use burrows and place their eggs in a chamber at least a metre underground. If no such burrow exists, and the birds are unable to find an unused Manx Shearwater or rabbit burrow for their use, they have to dig it

Left: Parent Puffins visit their youngster up to six times a day.

themselves. Standing only 25cm tall, Puffins sometimes dig 200cm into the soil, using both foot and bill as excavating tools, the former for the floor and the latter for the ceiling. For birds that are used to the freedom of "flying" under the sea and swimming in the ocean, this must be tough work. Both sexes dig the burrow. They then collect some soft furnishings such as feathers or strands of grass to place inside – though this extra effort seems pointless, since these materials are not used to line the nest but merely clutter up the inside, like unwanted Christmas presents.

The next chore is incubation. Although Puffins lay only a single egg, it is quite a large one, and needs plenty of warmth to keep it on the road to hatching. In fact, a good many Puffins fail the test and lose their egg at this point. It's easy to look upon incubation as a passive process, something you might be able to do whilst watching TV, for instance. But in fact eggs need to be turned every so often, and the act of using body heat to keep them warm actually drains significant amounts of energy from the birds. Furthermore, the parents incubate the egg in shifts averaging 32 hours, which is a long time to be stuck in a burrow.

If all goes well, the egg hatches after about 40 days. There is no time for a break, of course, because chicks are even more demanding than eggs, and complain more noisily too. Although the parents only deliver fish to the youngster about six times a day, which doesn't sound much, they have the same problem as other seabirds in feeding their young: there is no guaranteed food supply close at hand. Thus Puffins may travel as far as 100km to find food, and regularly venture 50km out from shore. This means that, in theory, they may get through 600km of flying a day – an extremely heavy burden for a plump bird with small wings that has to flap very fast to keep airborne.

Puffins are unusual among members of their family in chasing not single fish, but shoals, and their unique bills are specially adapted for holding a great number of small, writhing bodies at the same time. The mandibles are quite long, and the edges of the bill are fitted with small projections that point back towards the mouth and, with the help of the tongue, keep the fish in place. As a result Puffins often carry large loads of small fish, and there is one record of a bird carrying 62 in its bill at once.

One might imagine that carrying the more normal 10–20 fish back on a return journey of 50km is demanding enough. Once the birds approach their burrows they must be pretty tired,

and the last thing they want at this point is trouble. But the truth is, of course, that a Puffin bringing back fresh fish to port is an attractive sight for a lazy predator, and some hard-working parents find themselves intercepted by skuas and even other auks, and often lose their hard-earned catch.

All in all, the lot of a breeding Puffin is a tough and laborious one, and their 12–week season is a heavy challenge. By the end of their 40-day stint of feeding the young, it appears that the strain finally gets to them. Thus, for the last few days of its burrow life, the youngster receives no fish offerings at all, and it is hunger that eventually forces it to leave the nest site one night, quite alone and abandoned. The parents' hard work has at last paid off, but they don't see the fruits of their labours swimming past. They are probably too knackered, and are simply snoozing on the water, grateful for the long winter of recovery that lies ahead.

The bill of the Puffin is adapted for holding small fish crosswise, secured by the tongue.

The sixty-day father

MALE BIRDS tend to have a poor reputation as parents. This has probably been earned by such birds as ducks, for example, in which the males abandon their families as soon as the eggs hatch, or by Swallows, which fritter away time chasing after extra females when they should be feeding their young. As ever, of course, the damning headlines conceal a more complex picture. The truth is that a good many avian males are excellent, competent parents. Among garden birds, many help a great deal by feeding both female and young, and sweat hard in doing so.

But few parents of either sex are quite as devoted as the male Guillemot. This is a bird that takes fatherhood further than probably any other bird in the world. Both in time spent and distance travelled, the Guillemot is the coolest dad of all.

Guillemots are cliff-nesters that eat fish and live like sardines in a tin. Their colonies are the most densely packed of any bird in the world, with the parent birds living shoulder to shoulder on narrow, draughty ledges, often without enough room to turn around or stretch. Once the chicks hatch, one to each "nest", the pressure on space becomes even less bearable, making it difficult for the adult to land when it visits the chick to feed it, let alone to brood and take care of it. At the same time, once the youngster is about 20 days old, the parents begin to feel the strain of commuting back and forth from the cliff with their hard-earned catches. Something has to give.

Unfortunately for the chick, what gives is its tenure on the natal ledge. You might think that, for a bird accustomed to living on cliff ledges, a transfer from nesting site to sea would be simply routine. But remember: the chick is 20 days old. That means it is only thirty per cent the size of the adult. And it cannot fly; its flight feathers haven't developed. That, you might imagine, is a bit of a snag when a bird is contemplating a drop of 200m or more to the water below the cliff. All it can do is jump, and trust that its lightness, and outspread wing-stumps and feet, will cushion its fall.

The young Guillemot, then, faces a daunting challenge very early in life. Not only is the jump from the cliff perilous in itself, but young Guillemots of about three weeks old make handy snacks for gulls and skuas, whose presence is a constant menace to seabird colonies. The jump isolates the chick from its parents, if only momentarily, thus handing an opportunity

Too young to fly …

… but too old to stay. The youngster jumps.

to these deft predators, who may snatch the fledgling as it launches into the air, or field it from the sea when it lands.

This, though, is where the Guillemot super-dad comes in. Its ability to protect the chick is, let's face it, quite limited, but it has a major role to play in encouraging the chick to leave the ledge and thus preventing it from starving to death. When the time comes for the youngster to plunge, which is always at twilight on a fine evening, the father begins to play this important role. He starts by making loud, so called "leap" calls, pleading with his chick to go. He also repeatedly performs a special bowing display, pointing his bill somewhat unsubtly towards the sea, in case there should be any misunderstanding.

Most chicks don't leap straight from their breeding ledge, but walk to traditional dropping off points, often some distance away, with their father in close attendance. Once they arrive they have, of course, crossed a threshold and cannot turn back. But still the father gives the leap-call, and keeps on bowing; if necessary he will preen the chick and the two will fence bills playfully. Strengthened by paternal confidence, the fledgling jumps.

This manoeuvre – though imperative for survival – looks like suicide, yet within seconds the fledgling has immersed itself in its most natural habitat, the sea. Landing with a belly-flop, the chick has little time to regroup. It faces immediate and acute danger from gulls and skuas, many of which are mature birds that have learned to keep an eye out for Guillemot plunges and have honed their skills in finding the tiny blobs floating in the inky evening swell. The chick can take some evasive action from them, diving below the surface to get away from these more limited swimmers, but this can only buy it time. Its most important need is to find its father. Without making contact with the older bird, the chick will be doomed.

The father has also dived down towards the sea, just a second or two after its youngster. Having landed somewhat more gracefully, as befits a fully-feathered bird, the adult now begins to call incessantly as it searches for its

offspring. Both birds recognise each other's calls, but against the noise of the sea, the cackling and wailing of the gulls, and the plaintive cries of any number of other Guillemot duos, there is no guarantee that they will be successful.

If birds feel relief, Guillemots must do so when they hear a familiar voice in this terrifying environment. Reunited, the two birds kick their legs and move quickly away from the deadly melee around the base of the cliff. It will not be long before they reach the safety of deeper water. Both father and chick dive repeatedly as they swim out into the night. The gulls won't chase them; they can find easier pickings among the lost and confused chicks around the cliffs. As the land becomes more and more distant, the two Guillemots will have their patch of water to themselves.

Despite its dramatic stunt, this chick, remember, is still very much a fledgling. It has only experienced the water for a few hours and, although it knows innately that it must dive to catch food, it has no skill in doing so. For many days the chick will be dependent on its father supplying the fish, until, under what is effectively an apprenticeship, it learns the art of snatching this elusive prey for itself. Overall, father and child stay together for up to sixty days, swimming far out to sea on their long fishing expedition. The two birds may cover 700km before, at last, they part.

You might wonder, amidst all this drama, what the female parent is up to while her chick embarks on life's adventures. Well, she is no slouch, and contributed her fair share of fish to the youngster while it was on the ledge. The effort of producing the egg, though, leaves her much weaker than her partner, and the feeding/swimming marathon is probably beyond her remaining reserves of energy. So instead, she rests on the home ledge and, after a week or two, goes out to sea to moult. She cannot contribute to the chick's welfare and, of course, will have no knowledge of what fate befalls it. But she will probably get back together with the same mate next season. Who knows whether he can or will divulge the news?

But one thing the female Guillemot does know. Her chick will be looked after by perhaps the best father in the avian world.

Together alone – father and child on the high seas.

143

Scare tactics by Skuas

IT MUST be agony. Imagine that you have been to the shops to buy an expensive gift, battled the crowds for an hour or two to obtain it, and then got caught in traffic on your way home. You finally reach your doorstep, exhausted but flushed with success, only to find, to your horror, that someone has been waiting for you. Someone very menacing. Terrified, you hand over your treasured item. It's only when the shock of being mugged has waned that you begin to realise that your whole afternoon of effort and hassle has been in vain. You have had double trouble: you have been both threatened and robbed, and it is a deeply unsettling and dispiriting experience.

Let's hope this never happens to you. But spare a thought, meanwhile, for a number of our cliff-nesting seabirds, which endure a similar experience quite frequently. These birds, unfortunate creatures that they are, have become the victims of the sea cliff's arch troublemakers, the skuas. If skuas weren't around, life would be much easier for everyone.

A dive-bombing raid by an Arctic Skua.

Skuas are quite scarce breeding birds in Britain, being almost entirely confined to Scotland, especially the northern isles. There are two species, the Great Skua and the Arctic Skua. Both are similar in appearance to gulls, their close relatives, but if anything they have even sharper and more powerful bills, and their feet are equipped with a unique combination of webs for swimming and claws for stabbing and eviscerating. This makes skuas highly dangerous and well worth avoiding. Like many muggers, their chief hunting ploy is intimidation, but their threats are never phoney; they have the means to kill, and will do so without scruple when required.

And many birds do suffer this fate. Our smaller seabirds, especially Puffins and Kittiwakes, often fall prey to Great Skuas, which may harvest them in large numbers. And although Arctic Skuas eat mostly fish and – on their Arctic breeding grounds – rodents such as lemmings, they too are capable of killing small birds such as waders, and of taking the eggs and chicks of just about anything.

But it is the skuas' nuisance value, rather than their predatory behaviour, that probably has the most impact at seabird colonies. That's because they have cottoned on to the fact that, at a certain stage in the breeding season of just about every cliff-nesting bird, adults have to make fishing trips out to sea and return with their catch more or less intact, ready to present to the young. What easier tactic could there be for a confirmed pirate, therefore, than to make a living from stealing these deliveries? It cuts out a great deal of effort. All the skua needs to do is to intercept the food-carriers in a frightening enough way, and they will quickly drop their fish and fly off in terror, allowing the skua to swoop upon the bounty.

And that is exactly what they do, for weeks on end. It has been shown with Arctic Skuas, for example, that for the first week of their own chicks' life, they need to sustain their brood with at least some food obtained relatively legitimately. But for the second and third weeks, the young can be nourished entirely upon the Skuas' ill-gotten swag. And it has also been shown, hardly surprisingly, that they tend to time their breeding to synchronise with that of their most frequent victims. So when Arctic Terns or Puffins are feeding their young, the Arctic Skuas are doing the same.

A skua attack, for all its underhand motives, is nonetheless riveting to watch. The attacker usually attempts to surprise its victim, so it will often fly low over the sea towards it, with fast, deep wing-beats reminiscent of an accelerating hawk, and then suddenly rush at it from below. Sometimes the quarry is so shocked by this that it drops its delivery straight away, but more often it shows a little more determination, grimly holding on to the fish and trying to give the skua the slip. But skuas, with their aerodynamic form and highly manoeuvrable flight, are very difficult to shake off. They can "lock on" to a bird in front, following each twist and turn, while gradually overhauling their target. Chases may continue for several minutes, and when this happens – especially when two or more skuas join in the fun – the fish-carrier is usually worn down.

Reaching the end – a Gannet finally disgorges its catch.

Grudgingly it relinquishes the hard-earned catch to its pursuer, which gleefully fields it from the sea or catches it in mid-air.

The skua doesn't always win. Some birds are simply too tenacious, or the skua makes a mistake, or the potential victim is already too close to home for the chase to succeed. Some birds, such as Fulmars, may simply head for the open sea and shake the skua off this way. Studies on skua-tormented puffin colonies reveal that the fish carriers get away in at last one-fifth of cases and sometimes up to a third, depending on how far out from the cliff the attack started. They also show that a Puffin can expect to be intercepted on one of out every 25 deliveries it makes to its chick.

Puffins are relatively easy birds to spook, but skuas sometimes have to use quite different tactics to steal from other birds. Fulmars, for example, are more likely to be worn down than to be shocked into submission. And Gannets? Well, these are large birds, which means that only Great Skuas are big enough to dare challenge them. Their tactics are bruising indeed.

If you think about it, the very last thing a Gannet wants to see on its return to the nest-site is a skua. This is a bird that, for a single delivery to its off-spring, might have made a return trip of 350km to the catch-and-carry, so the prospect of losing its goods at the last moment to an

undeserving pirate is an anathema. But the Great Skua is well prepared for the Gannet's fighting mood, and the battle between the two, therefore, can be epic – like a seabird version of King Kong versus Godzilla. Not only is there chasing and harassing, as with other birds, but physical violence too, the skua barging and grabbing at the Gannet's feathers, and the Gannet returning in kind. Frequently, the pirate grabs a wing of the larger bird, tipping it into the sea, where, like many a good movie scrap, the tussle might finish with both bedraggled birds up to their necks in water.

Back on land, where their nests are placed on the ground in moorland, skuas are tender parents. They may feed their young off the back of others, but their care for their offspring is as great at anyone else's. And, like any other bird, skuas too can be threatened at the nest and find themselves suddenly vulnerable. They have predators, too.

But they also have weapons. And, if you, as a potential predator, should stray into the territory of a pair of skuas, you will quickly find yourself their target. They will dive-bomb you repeatedly and, in contrast to most other birds, can actually cause you harm. Skuas usually lead with their feet, and if their claws catch you, they can easily draw blood. The experience, though not fatal, will certainly be unpleasant and intimidating.

So just thank your stars you're not a Puffin!

THE OPEN SEA

Hidden depths

WE CAN easily appreciate the sea's differing moods, from its brooding quiet to its outbursts of surf-scattering fury. But whatever its mood, it always seems to be a blanket of uniformity, encompassing miles and miles of the same waves, unbroken by land, that make patterns and conduct watery conversations entirely amongst themselves. The birds that make their living here face a never-ending task of picking holes in this blanket. Beneath it lie the scattered concentrations of food that allow them to survive.

NOT ALL OF Britain is land. Sitting on a boat tens of kilometres out to sea, you might be surrounded by water, but you are still within the compass of the British Isles. And though the birds passing by may seem unfamiliar, they are no less British than the Robins on your spade. The only difference is in the perception we have of them.

But this perception, nonetheless, reflects the reality of our experience. We do not live out here, and the birds that do are by and large not very well known to us. We see them at their colonies when, once a year, they visit land to breed, and scientists have gathered plenty of knowledge and statistics about their brief stay on solid ground. But it is out at sea, far from land, that seabirds are most completely at home. And it is here that we metaphorically lose their scent as they lead lives that we know very little about. Only recently, using satellite tracking, have scientists begun to reveal the hidden details of seabirds' lives on the ocean wave.

Looking for clues

Perhaps the most obvious mystery about birds on the oceans is how they actually find the food that they need. We know plenty about how they catch it. Simple observation tells us, for example, that Gannets and terns plunge into the sea from a height to catch fish; that Storm Petrels and Kittiwakes can flit down and scoop food from the surface without missing a wing beat; that Fulmars and shearwaters can swim on the surface and bend down to catch surface-living food; and that auks, Cormorants and seaducks dive down from a swimming position to catch what they need underwater.

But what is much less clear is how they locate this food in the first place. Food in the sea is never uniformly distributed; it forms localised concentrations that may be tens of kilometres, or even more, apart. This means that, if you swim or fly for a hundred kilometres in a straight line, you might chance upon an area of plenty, but you might miss it altogether. There is also the problem of the watery medium. The surface of the sea only ever hints at what is below, and it can be difficult to read by eye even if you are professional seabird. This makes locating food far more difficult than it is on land.

How, then, do seabirds forage successfully? After all, they are faced with two challenges: first, finding the right patch of sea; and second, locating where the actual food is within it – the right patch within the patch, so to speak.

Meeting these challenges first requires a thorough reconnaissance over the right part of the ocean. Each species searches over a different "hot" area, depending on its diet and feeding technique. A good many seabirds could perhaps be more

Previous spread: Manx Shearwaters and Kittiwakes effortlessly ride an ocean storm.

Left: The black wing-tips of the ocean-going Kittiwake give the impression the bird has been flying over ink.

We can't see anything special about this patch of sea – but these Common Scoters (a sort of duck) know there are mussel beds just below.

appropriately described as coastal birds because their hot areas are either close to the shore, or at least over the continental shelf, where the depth does not exceed 200m and is usually considerably less. Such species as Gannets, Guillemots, Cormorants and seaducks fall into this category. In this relatively shallow water prey can be quite predictable, and the birds may even be able to feed on the seabed.

Going deeper

Further out, things become trickier. The water is deeper, and thus the influence of the seabed is reduced, although not absent. Birds tend to concentrate around areas where one type of water meets another. This happens, for example, when sea currents, which are forever racing across the globe, meet relatively still water or hit other currents at so-called "fronts". The mixing and churning of the currents brings up nutrients from deeper water or from the seabed. These nutrients allow plant plankton to grow, which in turn attracts animal plankton. The seabirds either feed directly on this plankton, or upon those animals that it nourishes lower down the food chain.

Agitations where currents collide are not the only sea features to attract birds. The varied topography of the seabed also ensures that churning and upwellings occur here and there, and can be exploited. A good example is at the edge of the continental shelf, where the seabed drops off into the depths and there is inevitably a disruption to the flow of water. Many of the most oceanic of the seabirds, such as Storm Petrels, concentrate at places like this. Other potential hot areas include eddies formed far offshore where land has disrupted the flow of a current, and the plumes of freshwater caused by rivers pouring their contents into the sea. None of these features is necessarily visible to the birds, but experience, or the

experience of their peers, ensures that they at least begin their search in the right part of the ocean.

On a more local level, having located a hot area, the trick again seems to be to find places where the sea is not entirely uniform, where it seems just a little more churned up than normal. Again, the small effects of local currents and upwellings can show seabirds the way. These are known as "streaks", and they may contain much more food than parts of the ocean only a few metres away. Streaks may be visible as stains of differently coloured sea, foamy patches or areas of stronger waves. They may also be formed simply by the action of high winds – a small but significant compensation for birds that have been previously buffeted by gales.

Streaks starkly exhibit another attribute of the ocean scene that makes food so hard to find, and that is its transitory nature. The seas and oceans are a dynamic and unfathomably complex system, and subject to the vagaries of wind and weather. This means that features are often short-lived and unpredictable; some last minutes, others days and others months. No amount of foreknowledge is available for many features of the seascape, so birds have to be alert for clues whenever they flicker into existence.

Sea creatures

Another ephemeral but useful feature of the ocean-scape is the periodic surfacing of predatory fish and mammals. Many schooling fish are as migratory as birds, and their fast-moving, continually travelling shoals tend to attract a retinue of hangers-on, notably larger fish and dolphins. As with any commotion over the vast open seas, these disturbances attract attention – seabirds might spot the fins of dolphins, for example – and can lead foraging species such as Fulmars and shearwaters toward rich pickings.

149

Fulmars bicker and fuss in the wake of a pilot whale.

of their wake, but others provide the immense attraction of bringing food straight to the surface. Studies have shown that some seabirds can even distinguish between fishing boats and merchant ships!

Trawlers invariably have a following of seabirds scrapping after the discarded fish and offal, including Fulmars, Gannets, gulls and skuas. These scrums are seldom disappointed, but in truth fleets of trawlers are a mixed blessing. They are, after all, competing with birds, and over-fishing has critically compromised seafood populations for birds, just as it has for humans.

World travellers

Of course, no seabird could possibly take advantage of fleeting events on the water surface unless it was capable of long-distance travel, and the serendipity that this allows. Although some birds of continental shelf waters, such as seaducks and auks, can get where they need to go by

Whales, too, must surface regularly, and the very fact that they may be rising from great depths – bringing with them a rich upwelling of plankton-filled water – presents yet another opportunity for waiting seabirds. Some may follow whales and dolphins for many hours at a time.

We human beings are also, of course, major predators of seafood. We tend to do it from ships, however, and it would take a rather unobservant seabird not to notice these from time to time and clock their potential usefulness. Some ships are of limited worth, offering nothing but the churning

150

swimming, the majority rely on flight. And they can certainly fly a long way. The Manx Shearwater, for example, which breeds entirely in the north-east Atlantic, travels during the non-breeding season to the waters off southern South America, some 10,000km away, where the fishing is better. Elsewhere in the world, some albatrosses and shearwaters travel that far simply to find food for young in the nest!

These oceanic wanderers are well designed for long-distance flight. Most have long, narrow wings that are ideal for creating lift (lift is generated along the whole wing, so it increases with wing length), but also require the bird to move forward quite rapidly in order to prevent stalling. In the windy conditions that tend to prevail at sea, it is easy to move forward quickly, so seabirds can soar for many hours with scarcely a wing-beat. The sea also offers its own special form of help. The action of wind and waves creates ideal conditions for "slope-soaring", in which a bird will simply ride the small updrafts created by a moving wave. And, in slightly stormier conditions many species will practise "dynamic soaring", in which a bird flying well above the sea can glide slowly down towards the surface with the wind behind, and then quickly double back into the wind to allow itself to be whisked up again, repeating the process *ad infinitum*. Birds can simply flip between dynamic soaring and slope-soaring at will, using the energy of wind and sea, rather than their own energy, to commute vast distances.

Another important adaptation of seabirds is their ability to drink seawater. However impressive your flying skills, you cannot get the best out

The long, narrow wings of the Manx Shearwater allow it to glide for long periods, so long as there is sufficient wind.

of the sea if you have to keep returning to land to satisfy your thirst. So, in addition to the fluids that naturally occur in their fishy diet, seabirds also drink a great deal and – unlike the Ancient Mariner – are perfectly able to utilise the water that they take on board. All seabirds, including seaduck, have special glands whose job it is to secrete excess salt from the body fluids. These are usually found at the base of the eye.

Seabirds are also, by necessity, hardy and resilient creatures. On the whole, they have denser feathering than most other birds, and a less patchy, more even covering. This keeps them well insulated, whatever the wind or waves may throw at them. Below the skin they also keep a permanent layer of fat, which essentially acts as an energy reserve that they can draw upon if feeding is interrupted for more than a few days.

Riding the storm

And of course, feeding often is interrupted. Our seabirds live in a world where storms and tempestuous seas are a regular fact of life. They must be able to ride out fierce winds, or at least avoid the worst fury of the sea. And they must be able to do this by night and day, and then get straight back to the serious business of feeding as soon as the disturbance passes.

Not surprisingly, we know very little about how birds ride out ocean storms because we cannot usually observe them doing it – at least, not if we value life and limb! But we do know that bad weather does affect seabirds. Some are known to make for the eye of a storm, where the weather is calmer, and maintain position there; others have been seen apparently using escape routes around a deep depression. Many, we can be reasonably certain, keep their head down by flying low into the troughs between waves, where the wind has less purchase upon them.

But bad weather does inevitably produce casualties. A few seabirds, especially auks and Leach's Petrels, are periodically forced by long-lasting, severe weather systems onto coastlines and occasionally even inland. These events are known, appropriately, as "wrecks". They are as devastating to these marine birds as the wreck of a ship is to human landlubbers, since on land they cannot find enough food and, already weakened by their ordeal, cannot compete with the local birds.

Wrecks can be exciting happenings for birdwatchers, since they allow a close-up view of these oceanic sprites. And that, of course, is a rare privilege. For these are truly strange and exotic wanderers, whose lives, even today, remain shrouded in mystery.

The Gannet's nose-dive

IT MUST be terrifying to be a fish. True, fish do seem prone to panic, but even by their over-wrought standards an attack by a flock of Gannets must rate as pretty scary. One moment the fish are swimming along near the surface, minding their own business and enjoying the plankton; the next moment dozens of huge birds with dagger-like bills are plunging from the heavens in an air-raid, spearing the water and coming straight for them. The fish never know where the next attack will come from and so they swim at full throttle this way and that, soon becoming exhausted with the effort. Many perish, succumbing either to injury, oxygen deprivation or the digestive juices of a gannet.

Plunging Gannets may look terrifying from below, but from the surface the spectacle is nothing short of awesome – especially if you are watching from a boat and the birds are diving in all around you. A six-foot wingspan makes Gannets Britain's largest seabird, and their size tends to amplify everything they do. Normally, they fly rather low over the water, alternating bouts of slow wing-beats with long glides; but once they have fish in their sights, each bird rises well above the surface and scouts around at a height normally between ten and fifteen metres up. Once it has spied its prey, it hovers briefly or simply stalls. Then, with its head outstretched and its wings folded back so that their tips meet behind the tail, it plunges down towards the water, accelerating to a speed of about 110kph on impact, and enters with a satisfying splash.

Only recently, with the help of underwater

The excitement of Gannets and Dolphins reflects the panic below the water surface.

filming, have we learned exactly how Gannets capture their prey once they hit the water. It was originally thought, reasonably enough, that the scouting from above and the impetus of the dive would enable Gannets to fall straight upon their intended victim and grab it straight away – even to spear it with their bill. After all, Gannets often steer themselves during the dives to fine tune their aim, occasionally turning through 180 degrees or more before they finally hit the water. And there seems little doubt that they do sometimes hit their target directly. But the main purpose of the dive is simply to take them deeper into the water than they could reach by swimming down from the surface – right into the midst of the shoal. Only once submerged do they become hunters. Swimming with their wings, they have been reported as reaching depths of up to 23m.

Plunge-diving is feeding turned adventure sport, and Gannets have several special adaptations to cope with the extreme stresses involved. These include a network of large air sacs all over their body, fed by the respiratory system, which lie between the skin and muscle, and cushion the impact of the dive. When you are hitting the water from 45m up, as has been recorded, you need this level of shock-absorption. Also, a Gannet's nostrils don't open externally on top of the bill, as do those of most birds, but internally within the bill. When a Gannet enters the water it holds its bill tight shut, which has the rather obvious benefit of keeping the water out of its nose. Finally, the Gannet's long, slender wings give it the perfect manoeuvrability with which to perform its stunts.

Although Gannets can work on their own, it is more common for them to form flocks. Once one bird has detected a decent shoal of fish, it normally cannot keep its discovery quiet, even if it wanted to. Its diving and brilliant white plumage soon attract the attention of every Gannet in the vicinity, and a crowd quickly builds up. Soon each bird is feeding madly, and individuals often cross paths as they dive, giving the impression of a shower of feathered meteorites. With fulminating splashes coming every few seconds as the feathered missiles bombard the water from every angle, the spectacle has a frenzied feel.

This maelstrom is almost certainly intentional. While the birds may be following fast-swimming fish and must move quickly to keep up with them, and while they are undoubtedly quite desperate to make the most of a typically fleeting abundance of food, they still probably don't have to react with quite such as dizzying hustle. But it seems that a melee of strikes has the effect of unsettling the fish into swimming too fast and changing direction too often, thereby leaving them disorientated. Thus the Gannets' frenzied diving helps to disarm their prey. And the more birds, the greater the effect. In other words, the Gannets gain by hunting together; it is even possible that they deliberately co-ordinate their spectacular plunges.

Some scientists have suggested that the Gannet has its bold white plumage partly for this reason. Any birdwatcher will tell you that the Gannet is one of the easiest birds to spot at a great distance, especially on a dull day, and there is no question that these birds can see others of their kind at similar or possibly greater distances. If all the Gannets of an area were to spread out widely, but maintain distant visual contact, then it would enable them both to cover a very large patch of ocean and to come together quickly once food had been sighted. Vultures use the same technique on land: their dark forms silhouetted against the bright sky are visible to other vultures for miles, enabling them collectively to comb a vast area for food.

There is little doubt that this sort of searching does take place, in other white-coloured seabirds as well as Gannets. And let's face it: the plunging gannets hit the target with a bit more style than a pack of marauding vultures.

The water boils with well fed Gannets and Gulls.

The Guillemot can chase fish 100m below the surface.

Ventures into the deep

A GOOD many seabirds are hardly worth the name; they are far more aerial than marine, spending more of their life flying than they ever do on the sea. Some, such as Storm Petrels, simply flirt with the water, snatching items from the surface and barely ever getting their feet wet.

On the other hand, there are also plenty of seabirds that embrace the sea to the full. They land on it, swim about on it and dive below the surface to find their food in it. These, if you like, are the consummate seabirds: consuming from the water and thereby, in a way, being consumed by it.

But these aquatic experts don't have it easy. True, some birds – especially those that feed inshore – simply dive down to reach a reliable, stationary source of food, such as a bed of shell-fish. But these are the exception. Those birds that hunt in the open sea, especially deeper waters, face more of a challenge. Their prey moves about, and must be chased. And the sea tends to conspire against the chaser.

The first problem a seabird has to contend with is the gloom. You don't have to go far underwater before the light fades; even in clear water the intensity drops to 5% of its surface value at 100m down. British waters are, of course, seldom clear. Many of our species dive near the coast, where the action of waves, currents and tides makes conditions distinctly murky. The same applies near estuaries and many parts of the ocean further out. So the moment a bird submerges, it can find itself in the aquatic equivalent of a foggy night.

Nonetheless, birds often go a long way down. Shags, inshore fishing birds, have been recorded descending to 61m and Long-tailed Ducks, of similar ilk, to 55m. The auks, a family that includes the Puffin and Guillemot, go deeper still, well over 100m into the abyss. And even shearwaters, which are generally considered to be mostly surface-feeders, may sometimes descend 30m or more. None of these are trivial submergences and all plunge the birds ever deeper into the darkness.

Seabirds seem to overcome these problems by having exceptionally good vision. Most have large eyes, which allow plenty of light on to a retina packed with detecting cells. The larger the eye, the more detail they are able to see and the more light they can eke out of the difficult conditions. Seabirds' eyes are also adapted to flitting regularly between looking through air and looking through water, each of which has different refractive properties. This means that they can easily adjust their focus to objects at varying distances, making their eyes all the more effective

The Cormorant may swallow stones to reduce its buoyancy.

In common with the Cormorant, the Shag has specially modified feathers with little waterproofing, to help it dive.

underwater. Add to these abilities the fact that some potential prey may be bioluminescent (i.e. it creates its own light), then you get an idea of how seabirds work in the murk.

Another problem is that water is relatively dense, and requires considerable effort to work your way through. Most seabirds have solved this problem by using their most heavily powered organs, their wings, for thrust underwater – in other words, they effectively fly through it. Auks, shearwaters and most ducks fall into this category, as do the Fulmar and Gannet. However, there are exceptions: Cormorants, Shags, divers and grebes all propel themselves using their back-set feet, as do some seaducks of the shallows, including the Common Scoter and Scaup. Except for grebes, these deep divers are all powerful, heavily built species.

A similar problem is that birds in the sea are buoyant. Although this allows them to bob up easily when their search for prey is complete, it also means that for much of their dive they are invariably fighting against a return to the surface – and expending a great deal of energy in the process. But this problem isn't quite as restrictive as you might imagine. The deeper the dive, the more the buoyancy diminishes. This is because, at a certain level of water pressure, the air in a bird's lungs, air-sacs and plumage will reach the point where the bird's density matches that of the water. Below this point the bird will even begin to sink. So if a bird ensures that its dives reach the point of this so-called "neutral buoyancy", it will be able to save energy. The depth range of neutral buoyancy is quite narrow, so as soon as the birds rise above it they can bob easily back to the surface.

Cormorants and Shags have less of a buoyancy problem than other seabirds. Their bones are denser, and fitted with fewer air sacs and empty spaces, and their plumage is very unusual for an aquatic bird by dint of not being very waterproof – it lacks the feather structure that enables most birds to trap air, and instead absorbs water. So Cormorants and Shags can submerge with relative ease. Their only problem occurs when they have to return to land: they are forced to spend hours trying to dry out, with their wings characteristically spread as if on a washing line.

There is one final and insurmountable problem faced by diving birds: they can only survive underwater as long as their air supply lasts. They cannot act like Sperm Whales and spend over an hour in the depths. In fact, few seabirds can immerse for more than a couple of minutes. And ultimately, it is this inescapable reality that ties them to the surface. It ensures that seabirds – however impressive their diving skills – will always remain visitors rather than residents in the dark depths of the oceans.

Sniffing it out

BIRDS ARE renowned for their keen eyesight and hearing. In fact, many outperform us in both senses and, just to rub it in, they can also detect cues beyond our means, such as magnetic field and ultraviolet radiation. But lest we feel completely inferior, we outdo them in the area of taste, our buds numbering those of most birds by about 10,000 to 70, which evens things out a little.

Until recently, we also thought that we had a superior sense of smell. Birds, after all, have a relatively small olfactory bulb – the area of the brain responsible for smell – and thus a concomitantly low level of olfactory activity. And little in their behaviour suggests that birds are sensitive smelling creatures. You only have to whiff the stench in a used Kingfisher's nest, for example, to realise that the inhabitants must have some immunity to overpowering pongs just to be able to live there. But recent research into seabirds suggests that at least some birds are better equipped in that department than we once believed.

We have always known that the noses of Fulmars, Shearwaters and Storm Petrels are unusual. They are, after all, far more physically prominent than the noses of other birds, being placed atop the bill and encased in a horny tube that comprises two separate chambers, one for each nostril. This arrangement – often visible from some distance – has led this group of birds, technically known as Procellariformes, to acquire the nickname "Tubenoses". Although the tube-nose has long been known to carry out the unrelated function of directing secretions from the salt glands away from the eyes, nobody had previously thought that it might in any way have enhanced the birds' sense of smell.

Furthermore, many seabirds themselves are smelly. They don't just wear the scent of the sea, or collect whiffs from the fish and offal that they eat, but they actually have a distinctive musky aroma of their own. In other words, they have body odour. The smell pervades their plumage and seems to be spread when the birds are preening themselves, so it can be viewed as a definite, defining characteristic of certain species. It therefore seems reasonable to suppose that, since the birds give off a smell, they should also have the capacity to detect it. Some scientists have suggested that birds could follow a scent trail to their colonies, or even to their own individual nest-sites. One Alaskan species, the Crested

In the Fulmar, both nostrils open into a single tube along the top of the bill. It is possible that the tube may help to direct and concentrate smells to where they can be detected.

Auklet, has a strong smell of tangerine that can be detected from miles away. If we can detect it, then presumably so can the birds.

It is only now, though, that scientists are turning their attention towards a far more fundamental and useful function for smell in seabirds: the detection of food on the high seas. As we have seen, seabirds need all the help they can get in finding titbits on the relatively featureless oceanic surface, so having an extra sense to back up their eyesight could be more than a little handy. Added to this, the wind can blow unencumbered for hundreds of miles in the same direction over the waves, bringing olfactory cues with it, ripe for pursuit.

If you ever go on an oceanic field trip, you can often observe some pretty compelling evidence of seabirds using their noses. It is customary these days for the operators of such trips to bring along a concoction of fish fragments and smelly oil known as "chum" and toss it over the side, hoping to attract petrels. The effectiveness of this ploy is some evidence that the birds can sniff food out, although they could of course simply be coming to investigate some- thing they can see with their eyes. But experiments have also shown that the birds attracted almost invariably come from downwind and, as they do so, they don't follow a straight line, but describe a course of ever-decreasing zigzags. If they were following something seen, one might expect them to

A Storm Petrel follows a scent gradient.

make a bee-line for it, approaching as the crow flies. But if they were using an invisible scent trail, the zigzags would make more sense: they could only follow the trail by monitoring how the odour came and went as they crossed it. And, indeed, that seems to be what they are doing.

Over the last ten years a particularly interesting discovery has strengthened the case for seabirds having enhanced powers of smell: it is that certain foods significant to seabirds actually do smell, or at least their by-products do. And, furthermore, the birds seem to be attracted to the specific odour given off. What the scientists actually found was that plant plankton, when it is being eaten by animal plankton, emits a smelly chemical called dimethyl sulphide. It is this that attracts the birds, which in turn eat the animal plankton. And since, all over the world's oceans, animal plankton eats plant plankton as a matter of course, then following the smell of the dimethyl sulphide should, in theory, lead directly to lunch.

But despite all this evidence, we cannot immediately leap to the conclusion that seabirds follow their noses. Although a good sense of smell would seem a logical attribute for them, there are snags to the theory. For one thing, not all seabirds have an acute sense of smell and many species – including gulls, for example – show no behaviour that could be interpreted as scent-following at all. Furthermore, some species that definitely can smell well don't appear to follow the right chemicals in the expected way. Although this does not rule out the possibility that some seabirds use a sense of smell to help find food, it does raise a question about why – if scent is so important – not all of them do.

In this respect, as in so many others, the biology of seabirds remains a mystery.

Epilogue

This book, I hope, is as much as anything a celebration. It celebrates the star names and quirky characters among Britain's birds, and it celebrates the many and varied places where they live. In some ways you cannot separate one from another: all our birds fit neatly into their habitats, and their habitats would not be the same without them. We can appreciate them together, intertwined.

One thing that I hope strikes you reading this book, though, is the sheer diversity of habitats on our islands. Within our comparatively small area is a surprising range of landscapes and climates, all squeezed together with almost impertinent proximity, and ornithologically it is remarkable that we can hold both sun-loving birds such as Cirl Buntings and tough cookies like Ptarmigans on one single island. This is one of the delights of British birdwatching.

Another of the delights is that, as a reader, you can have a voice about British birds. Here on our island we have some of the most powerful conservation organisations in the world, who enjoy enormous popular support; among them are the RSPB, whom I am delighted endorsed this book. These days – almost incredibly, compared to just a short time ago – politicians listen to these organisations. So if you like British birds you are one of many, and there are those who speak on our behalf.

And that's just as well, because there will always be conflicts over land and its use. There are always people who wish to build roads or houses on wildlife-rich sites, for example, and on our farms commercial pressures have all but squeezed the birds out. All of the habitats mentioned in this book, with their special residents, are dependent on us for their maintenance and protection.

I hope, therefore, that this book will enhance your delight of the birds around you. And I also hope that it helps in some small way to swell the ranks of those who wish to see our wild places safeguarded for the future.

Acknowledgements

This book is the second in a series, so first I would like to thank Nigel Redman at A&C Black for commissioning the first one and keeping faith with the same team to do the follow-up.

My thanks to Mike Unwin for doing all the hard work of editing, and to long-suffering Julie Bailey for keeping the whole project together with good humour and forbearance. Meanwhile, Paula McCann managed the very tricky task of designing the look of the thing with great style.

Thanks to Peter Partington, artist extraordinaire. Peter, I couldn't have imagined that you would surpass your own high standards, but you have.

Finally, every writer needs an understanding family, and in Carolyn (wife) and Emily and Samuel (children) I have just that. (They even coped with me writing some of this book while on holiday in Australia). To you I give my thanks, and I love you all.

Bibliography

Alerstam, T. 1990. *Bird Migration*. Cambridge University Press.

Brooke, M. 2004. *Albatrosses and Petrels across the World*. Oxford University Press, Oxford.

Brown, A. and Grice, P. 2005. *Birds in England*. T & AD Poyser, London.

Brown, L. 1976. *British Birds of Prey*. New Naturalist Series. Collins, London.

Coombes, F. 1978. *The Crows – a Study of the Corvids of Europe*. B.T. Batsford, London.

Cramp, S. and Simmons, K.E.L. (eds.) 1977-83. *Handbook of the Birds of Europe, the Middle East and North Africa: The Birds of the Western Palearctic, Vols 1-3*. Oxford University Press, Oxford.

Cramp, S. (ed.) 1985-92. *Handbook of the Birds of Europe, the Middle East and North Africa: The Birds of the Western Palearctic, Vols 4-6*. Oxford University Press, Oxford.

Cramp, S. and Perrins, C.M. (eds.) 1993-94. *Handbook of the Birds of Europe, the Middle East and North Africa: The Birds of the Western Palearctic, Vols 7-9*. Oxford University Press, Oxford.

del Hoyo, J., Elliott, A. and Sargatal, J. (eds) 1992-2001. *Handbook of the Birds of the World, Vols 1-7*. Lynx Edicions, Barcelona.

del Hoyo, J., Elliott, A. and Christie, D.A. (eds) 2003-2004. *Handbook of the Birds of the World, Vols 8-9*. Lynx Edicions, Barcelona.

Ehrlich, P.R., Dobkin, D.S., Wheye, D. and Pimm, S.L. 1994. *The Birdwatcher's Handbook*. Oxford University Press, Oxford.

Elphick, C., Dunning, J.B. (Jr) and Sibley, D. 2001. *The Sibley Guide to Bird Life and Behaviour*. Christopher Helm, London.

Ferguson-Lees, J and Christie, D.A. *Raptors of the World*. 2001. Helm Identification Guides. Christopher Helm, London.

Fjeldså, J. 2004. *The Grebes*. Oxford University Press, Oxford.

Fuller, R.J. 1982. *Bird Habitats in Britain*. T & AD Poyser, London, Calton.

Gaston, A.J. 2004. *Seabirds: A Natural History*. T & AD Poyser, London.

Gibbons, D.W., Reid, J.B. and Chapman, R.A. (eds) 1993. *The New Atlas of Breeding Birds in Britain and Ireland: 1988-1991*. T & AD Poyser, London.

Harrison, C.J.O. and Castell, P. 1998. *Collins Field Guide to Bird Nests, Eggs and Nestlings of Britain and Europe*. Revised edition. HarperCollins, London.

Holden, P. and Cleeves, T. 2002. *RSPB Handbook of British Birds*. Christopher Helm, London.

Michl, G. 2003. *A Birders' Guide to the Behaviour of European and North American Birds*. Gavia Science.

Newton, I. 1972. *Finches*. New Naturalist Series. Collins, London.

Perrins, C. 1979. *British Tits*. New Naturalist Series. Collins, London.

Perrins, C. 1987. *Collins New Generation Guide: Birds of Britain and Europe*. Collins, London.

Perrins, C (ed). 2003. *The New Encyclopedia of Birds*. Oxford University Press, Oxford.

Simms, E. 1990. *Woodland Birds*. New Naturalist Series. Collins, London.

Snow, B. and Snow, D. 1988. *Birds and Berries*. T & AD Poyser, Calton.

Snow, D.W. and Perrins, C.M. (eds) 1998. *The Birds of the Western Palearctic*. Concise edition (2 vols). Oxford University Press, Oxford.

Turner, A. and Rose, C. 1994. *A Handbook to the Swallows and Martins of the World*. Christopher Helm, London.

Tyler, S.J. and Ormerod, S.J. 1994. *The Dippers*. T & AD Poyser, London.

Wernham, C.V., Toms, M.P., Marchant, J.H., Clark, J.A., Siriwardena, G.M. and Baillie, S.R. (eds) 2002. *The Migration Atlas: Movements of the Birds of Britain and Ireland*. T & AD Poyser, London.

Index